The Gospel of John

GOD'S WORD TODAY VI

A New Study Guide to the Bible

John F. O'Grady

The Gospel of John

Testimony
of the Beloved Disciple

PUEBLO PUBLISHING COMPANY
NEW YORK

Nihil Obstat :   *Rev. John Roos, STL, JCD*
                     Censor Librorum

Imprimatur :   ✠ *Howard J. Hubbard*
                     Bishop of Albany
                     August 31, 1982

Design: Frank Kacmarcik, D.F.A.

ISBN: 0-916134-35-0

Printed in the United States of America

CONTENTS

To Paul Francis McLaughlin

PREFACE

Interest in the Scriptures continues to grow. Men and women individually and in groups read, reflect on, discuss, pray from the Bible. I have taught, led, participated in such groups. This participation has convinced me that, despite all the worthwhile material on the Bible already available, there are still gaps to be filled for those people who truly care about the Bible but have had little or no preparation to extract its riches.

Several excellent guides to the Bible exist in the format of booklet series in which each volume provides commentary and explanation on a separate book of the Bible. However, for someone becoming acquainted with the Bible, to work through each book one by one can be a formidable task.

Other books focus on themes and main ideas distilled from the whole Bible. As valuable as such theologies and overall views are, there is still a need for a familiarity with the *text* of the Bible itself.

In this series, substantial portions of the Scriptures—extensive enough to convey style, language, tone—are the indispensable starting point. Essential background and explanation are provided and the lasting import of the text is suggested. Possibilities for individual or group reflection are offered.

When the reader has completed this series, he will have encountered many themes and main ideas, and this through a selected and guided reading of the text itself. This overall view can be filled in by further study of the individual books of the Bible.

The general plan emerges from a listing of the titles in this series. It is my strong recommendation that anyone using the series begin with Volume I. If the principles presented there are grasped, the spadework will be done for understanding what follows.

"Indeed, God's word is living and effective, sharper than any two-edged sword. It penetrates and divides soul and spirit, joints and marrow; it judges the reflections and thoughts of the heart" (Hebrews 4. 12).

Emil A. Wcela
Series Editor

FOREWORD

For several years I have been fortunate enough to have studied and taught the Gospel of John. Each time I read it, I come away with something of value that I have not experienced before. Like all books of the Bible, this gospel has its own depth which seems to recede further as a person digs deeper.

The need for all Christians to read and reflect on the gospels has become more evident in recent years. The Church cannot neglect its obligation to help believers to grow in a personal understanding of faith. What better way than a study of the Bible.

This series hopes to respond to that need and this volume in particular studies the Fourth Gospel, picking and choosing those themes that might prove helpful to the contemporary believer.

The insights that I have discovered and have tried to present in this book have come from personal reflection, from reading as well as from teaching and discussing with interested students. No effort to document the ideas has been attempted. The bibliography at the conclusion will help the reader who wishes more information.

I hope that the love I have for this particular gospel and the community that stands behind it will be evident in what I have written and will encourage others to join me. The Gospel of John has helped believers for centuries. May this book help believers to allow the gospel itself to guide them.

John F. O'Grady
Monterey, Massachusetts, 1981

CHAPTER I

THE BACKGROUND
OF THE GOSPEL

The Gospel of John is the Word of God directed to God's people today. By means of this gospel we can gain some insights into our common Christian heritage and receive some guidance for our personal religious life. This gospel is like the other gospels in that it tells of the life and death of the Lord but has so many distinctive approaches to the reality of Jesus that it has to be separated from the other three gospels and studied on its own with its own peculiar theology and its particular approach to Christianity.

When anyone studies a book of the Bible decisions must be made on precisely what aspect or what part of the book should be examined. Since we deal with the Word of God the rich depth of meaning will never be exhausted. We learn but never reach a sense of total understanding. Surely that is true when we examine the Gospel of John. The richness of faith expressed in this book far surpasses any human effort to control and understand. For this reason, we shall pick and choose those elements which might prove helpful to the contemporary Christian in his or her journey in faith to the Lord.

A SECULAR APPROACH TO CHRISTIANITY

The word secular does not always have the best connotation. It emphasizes this world, the present reality, and centers on human relationships. No great interest is directed to the spiritual world, the future reality, or to a relationship with God. Surprisingly so, the Gospel of John is secular: it emphasizes this world, the present reality, and human relationships.

The Synoptic gospels and the writings of Paul speak often of the other world, the future hopes, expectations, and eternal life that is to come. But for the author of the Gospel of John, salvation and eternal life is now: "Eternal life is this: to know you, the only true God, and him whom you have sent, Jesus Christ" (Jn 17. 3). "The man who hears my word and has faith in him who sent me possesses eternal life. He does not come under condemnation, but has passed from death to life" (Jn 5.24). The emphasis is on the present life in which a person has already been judged and has already begun to experience eternal life. This world counts.

HUMAN RELATIONSHIPS

The gospel is also secular in its emphasis on human relationships. The Synoptics have the twofold love of God and love of neighbor as the fundamental commandment of Jesus (Mk 12. 30; Mt 22. 34-40; Lk 20. 39-40). The Gospel of John no longer speaks of a love of God and neighbor but only the new commandment that Jesus gives: the love of the brethren (Jn 13. 34). If people love one another, then they have fulfilled the command of the Lord: the love of the brethren fulfills the command to love God but the emphasis focuses on the love of the brethren: human relationships are primary. No wonder that from this same community can come the First Letter of John with its admonition: "One who has no love for the brother he has seen cannot love the God he has not seen" (1 Jn 4. 20).

CHURCH AND SACRAMENTS

The understanding of the Christian Church presupposes an authority as well as the celebration of the sacraments. Without the clear line of authority that ultimately binds the leaders of the Church to Jesus, the Church would not survive in a world that too often appears filled with evil and sin. Also, without the celebration of the sacraments, in particular baptism and the eucharist, the Christian Church would no longer exist. Other elements interact to create a sense of Church but without the sense of authority and the celebration of the sacraments it would be difficult to identify the Church.

The Gospel of Matthew has a clear line of authority in its last chapter: "Full authority has been given to me both in heaven and on earth; go, therefore, and make disciples of all the nations. Baptize them in the name 'of the Father, and of the Son, and of the Holy Spirit.' Teach them to carry out everything I have commanded you. And know that I am with you always, until the end of the world" (Mt 28. 18-20).

Luke also established authority in his prologue by joining his tradition to eyewitnesses to Jesus (Lk 1. 1-4). The pastoral epistles also have authority coming from Paul to Timothy (2 Tim 1. 6-14). Luke also in his Acts of the Apostles established a hierarchy of *presbuteroi, episcopoi* and *diaconoi* (elders, overseers, deacons).

The early Church quickly realized that survival demanded authority. The Church needed teachers who could give clear guidance and direction as the early community settled in, awaiting the return of the Lord. Unless the lines of authority and responsibility could be clearly drawn the Church would suffer from a diffusion of roles and the unity that Jesus had desired would be lost in individual claims and rival groups.

3

The Gospel of John, however, shows no great interest in this need for authority. There is no sending out of the apostles with the authority of Jesus during his ministry as found in the Synoptics (Mt 10. 5; Lk 9. 1). The Twelve are mentioned in the Johannine gospel only on two occasions: in chapter 6. 67-71 where Jesus talks about them abandoning him and betraying him and in chapter 20. 24 in reference to Thomas, the one who doubted. Disciples are mentioned frequently, but this connotes anyone, male or female, leader or follower, who has come to accept Jesus in faith.

The only true leader in this gospel is Jesus who is described as the Good Shepherd (chapter 10). The only one who shares in this leadership quality of Jesus is the Spirit who will guide the followers of Jesus to all truth (Jn 16.16). If the members of the Johannine community have the Spirit, they saw little need for other teachers and guides.

In chapter 21 after the resurrection, Jesus does confer a pastoral ministry upon Peter when he commands the apostle to feed his lambs and sheep (Jn 21. 15-17). This, however, differs considerably from the rest of the gospel and must be seen as an appendix, added by the final editor of the gospel. We shall return to this chapter later.

No matter what opinion one may follow with regard to this final chapter, the reader of the gospel quickly becomes aware of the unusual attitude toward Church authority in this gospel: the Twelve are rarely mentioned; all are given the Spirit, no one shares in the authority of Jesus apart from Peter in chapter 21. Compared with the clear lines of authority from Matthew, Luke, and the pastorals as well as the epistles of Paul, the Gospel of John clearly de-emphasizes the role of authority in the Church.

4

THE SACRAMENTS: BAPTISM

The second element for our consideration is the sacraments of baptism and the eucharist. The Synoptics all mention that Jesus was baptized by John. The Gospel of John omits this event. It seems to be understood but is never mentioned. Chapter 3 which contains the reference to "water and the Spirit" in the discourse between Jesus and Nicodemus must be rethought as meaning baptism in the spirit, or faith in Jesus and not baptism by water. We shall also return to this in a later chapter.

THE EUCHARIST

This gospel has the longest section on the Last Supper but does not mention the institution of the eucharist. The author does offer eucharistic teaching in chapter 6. 51b-58 but still does not refer to the actual institution. This question has plagued commentators for centuries. Why would John omit such an important event and why would he place eucharistic teaching within the context of the bread of life discourse? At least we can be assured that the author seems to be interested in a different interpretation of the sacraments.

I do not wish to imply that the author is opposed to the Church, to its authority or its sacraments. Rather, the author seems to de-emphasize certain aspects of the Church in favor of others. We shall see that throughout this gospel the overriding theme will be the personal commitment in faith to Jesus and the love of the brethren. When these are present, then we have a community based on the gospel of the Lord. Without them, we are far from the teaching of Jesus. The author centers on meaning rather than on fact or ritual, on what is fundamental rather than on theories about the nature of the Church. Clearly this testimony is unusual.

THE CHRISTOLOGY OF THE FOURTH GOSPEL

In a later chapter we shall deal with Johannine christology
in greater detail. For the present, the reader should be
aware that we have a portrait of Jesus quite different
from that of the Synoptics. Jesus always seems to speak
as if he were the risen Lord. He knows everything: that
Nathaniel is under the fig tree (Jn 1. 48); that the Samaritan
woman had been married five times (Jn 4. 17); what will happen to him in his passion (Jn 18.4). Jesus never seems like the
itinerant preacher of the Synoptics but always speaks from
eternity. He was always with God (Jn 1. 1) and even while on
earth appears to remain with God (Jn 1. 18). Jesus never suf-
fers in this gospel. Unlike the Synoptics, the author narrates
no agony in the garden, but rather sees the passion as a tri-
umphant parade ending up with the glorification of Jesus on
the cross. The emphasis centers on the divine Jesus, always
with the Father, always doing what the Father wishes, always
living in two spheres: the divine and the human.

HISTORY IN THE FOURTH GOSPEL

Often in past studies of the gospels readers were encouraged to
view the Synoptics as more historical than the Gospel of John.
John was the more spiritual or theological gospel written after
long reflection on the mystery of Jesus. John then could for
theological reasons change some of the historical aspects of
the life of Jesus; for example, when did Jesus drive the money
changers and the animals out of the temple — at the beginning of his ministry (Jn 2. 13-22) or immediately before his
death (Mt 21. 12-13; Mk 11. 15-17; Lk 19. 45-46)? The pre-
sumption was always in favor of the Synoptics but if the
Synoptics have only one journey to Jerusalem and John has
several, who is to say which account is more accurate? The
Synoptics had to place the cleansing of the Temple before the
passion since that was the only time Jesus was in Jerusalem.
John had the option of several occasions. Also, when did
Jesus die? Did he die on Friday, the day after the Passover

meal (Synoptics), or did he die on the day of preparation when the paschal lambs were being slaughtered in the temple (Jn 18.28; 19.31)? Can anyone with surety claim one over the other?

Any false sense of attributing more history to the Synoptics than to John must be avoided. All of the gospels are filled with a creative remembering in which the actual facts are recalled within the context of faith and the experience of the early Church. The Gospel of John contains authentic remembrances of the historical Jesus, what he said and did but as told in a creative way to support and bolster faith. The author preserves history but in his own peculiar way.

THE ORIGIN OF THE GOSPEL

The actual origin and early history of this document remains in shadows. Many have offered their theories and many have disagreed. A growing consensus holds to a collection of miracle stories as the origin of the gospel. This collection would have emphasized the miraculous aspect of the life of Jesus and may even have concluded with the final verses of chapter 20: "Jesus performed many other signs as well—signs not recorded here—in the presence of his disciples. But these have been recorded to help you believe that Jesus is the Messiah, the Son of God" (Jn 20. 30-31).

Some authors also thought they could detect a written source behind the many speeches of Jesus as well as an additional source for the passion account. Others will trace the various discourses of Jesus to homilies delivered by the Beloved Disciple to his community. Still others believe that the gospel went through various stages of development, perhaps five, which culminated in the gospel as we know it.

The problem with any theory of origin is conjecture. The gospel shows signs of development and various stages of writing but that does not imply that we can accurately explain this development. For our purposes the general reader should be aware that the gospel shows signs of being "put together" by one or several editors and writers over an extended period of time.

RELATIONSHIP TO THE SYNOPTICS

The author of John does produce a gospel and so parallels exist between John and the other gospels. All have a ministry of the Baptist, all narrate a multiplication of the loaves and a healing of an official's son, and all have a Last Supper and the passion. Sometimes in the past, writers and readers of the gospel supposed that John wrote his gospel to supplement and complete the Synoptics. An examination of the gospel, however, shows no evidence for such a theory.

The differences are too evident to believe that John knew the Synoptics as written documents. The best that can be concluded on the relationship between John and the Synoptics is the existence of a similar oral tradition behind both the Synoptics and John. John wrote independently of the Synoptics. The similarities between John and Luke and, to a lesser degree, Mark, can be attributed to a crossover of traditions in the early oral development of the Jesus story. However one concludes the relationship between the gospels, no evidence exists that would imply that John wrote knowing all of the Synoptics and attempted to complete or supplement them.

INFLUENCES ON THE GOSPEL

Reading commentaries on the Gospel of John encourages the reader to believe that if there existed a possible influence on the Gospel of John, that possibility was actualized. Some scholars find gnostic influences in thought patterns of dualism, or the need for knowledge; Jewish speculation on Wisdom can account for ideas in the prologue as well as the discourse on the bread of life. No direct depend-

ence on Greek philosophy or Hellenistic thought can be
detected but surely the milieu of the time and place
would have allowed for some indirect influence. The
period allowed for a general exchange of Old Testament
thought, rabbinic Judaism, Qumran ideology as well as
Greek philosophy and inchoate gnosticism. If the author
and the community of the gospel lived in the midst of such
a diverse intellectual milieu, one would expect to discover
some indirect influences on the gospel. No one can conclude, however, that the gospel was the result of any one
of the above-mentioned thought currents.

TIME AND PLACE

Most commentators on the Gospel of John place its origin
toward the end of the first century probably in Syria. No
one can actually prove time and place but provided an
elastic time period of approximately fifteen years from
85 A.D. to 100 A.D. is accepted the general reader can
be satisfied. In the history of interpretation several lo-
cations have been suggested. Ephesus, Alexandria in
Egypt and Antioch in Syria have been mentioned. This
writer tends toward Syria because of the cosmopolitan
character of the city and the fact that it was a flourish-
ing Christian center. I also am inclined to date it early
within that fifteen year period to account for the diver-
gent viewpoints in this gospel when compared to other
New Testament literature.

AUTHOR

The author of the gospel will forever remain in shadow.
The more current opinion accepts the Beloved Disciple, not
to be identified with John the son of Zebedee and one of
the Twelve, as the founder of the community and the source
of the tradition that the gospel expresses. In all probability
he was not one of the Twelve. As I have already noted the
Twelve do not figure prominently in this gospel and the Be-

loved Disciple appears as the most faithful follower of the Lord in contrast to all others. While not one of the Twelve, he would have to have been an eyewitness to give credibility to the teaching that the gospel espouses. Unless the Johannine community could trace its tradition to the ministry of Jesus, the peculiar approach to Christianity contained in this document would have been open to attack as inauthentic. The Beloved Disciple as the founder of the community and source of its teaching and an eyewitness and follower of the historical Jesus protected the community from complete rejection by other Christian groups.

I believe that the Beloved Disciple was the source behind the gospel but that does not necessarily imply he was the author. Possibly he was responsible for the early stage of the gospel but at least one if not several other hands actually shared in the final composition. The comparison of chapter 20 and chapter 21 with its two endings shows at least a final editor responsible for the final chapter and possibly for the prologue and other insertions throughout the body of the gospel.

PROBLEMS WITHIN AND WITHOUT THE COMMUNITY

The Johannine community, like any other Christian community, faced serious problems from within and without. Chapter 9 shows evidence of the problem of expulsion from the synagogue which took place some time after 85 A.D. (Jn 9.22). Up to that period Christianity was considered another Jewish sect enjoying the protection of Roman law and as such containing members who floated between synagogue and church. The final break with Jewish tradition must have been most difficult for Jewish Christians, with anger and pain on all sides.

The portrayal of John the Baptist suggests that some of his followers were still alive at the time of the Gospel of John. Since they would have claimed that John the Baptist was the true messiah, the Johannine community would have been anxious to present John the Baptist as inferior to Jesus, the true messiah.

Docetism was also a problem. This early heresy maintained that the body of Jesus was unreal, and that the divine Jesus engaged in a type of charade masquerading as human. The emphasis on the reality of the body of Jesus in the ministry of Jesus (he thirsts, is hungry and tired, etc.) as well as after his resurrection (he eats with his disciples) would help counteract this tendency.

Gnosticism, an early heresy which preached salvation through knowledge, existed in its formative stages and although there are some gnostic influences on the gospel, the emphasis on salvation through the glorification of Jesus in his death directly opposed the gnostic tendency to preach salvation through knowledge.

Finally the community faced internal problems. Some appear to have accepted Jesus more as a miracle worker than the Son of God. They had a low christology. Others had a high christology as characterized by the prologue and those experiences of the all-knowing glorified Lord always existing with the Father.

Conflicts also existed centered on authority and the meaning of the sacraments. The Third Letter of John, verses 9-11, imply that other Christian communities had problems with the Johannine community. Since the approach to Christian faith as expressed in the gospel differs considerably from that of the developing Church, disagreements and dissension were inevitable.

UNRESOLVED QUESTIONS

After reading these brief introductory remarks the reader realizes that the gospel offers many unresolved questions.

In a brief study on the gospel not all of these will find a resolution and perhaps some never will. The Gospel of John portrays a fascinating interpretation of the meaning of Jesus that will always give guidance and light to the Christian Church. The author displays genius in reflecting and presenting what is basic to Christianity. The gospel remains as the final testimony of the Beloved Disciple and his community to the Church of all ages. The careful reading of this testimony can only enrich the follower of the Lord.

SUGGESTIONS FOR REFLECTION

1. Does the analysis of the gospel as a literary work add or detract from the more traditional approach to the gospel?

2. If the Gospel of John appears to be secular, what value does it offer to the contemporary Christian?

3. Does the approach of the gospel to the Church and sacraments give any insight into the meaning of the Church and sacraments?

4. Does gnosticism have any value? Would it appeal to people today?

5. How does the understanding of the origin of the gospel affect your understanding of inspiration? Has it altered your appreciation or not?

6. Why is the Fourth Gospel considered to be a gospel when it is so different from the other gospels?

7. Do the various problems that the Johannine community faced in its existence, continue to cause concern today? What problems particularly are strong and in need of being evaluated today in the Church?

8. How does the meaning of faith in the Fourth Gospel relate to your understanding of faith?

CHAPTER II

JESUS IN THE FOURTH GOSPEL

Christology attempts to systematize the meaning of Jesus of Nazareth. Like all theology, christology involves a human effort to understand faith in a way that will gather many strands together into a unified whole. In the past some authors attempted a christology and claimed that it represented the christology of the New Testament. But in fact there is no one unified christology of the New Testament. Each writer has his own approach to Jesus and so we end up with many christologies coming from many different authors and from many different communities. In this work we will treat only the christology of the Gospel of John.

Jesus figures prominently in the Gospel of John. His work and person form the heart of the gospel. The approach in John is distinctive. Frequently scholars have studied Johannine christology searching for the key to unlock the meaning and purpose of his distinctive approach. They studied the various titles used, the interplay between the human and the divine Jesus, the interaction of who Jesus was and what he did. As we study this gospel we will discover that the christology of John relates to his anthropology. Johannine approaches to Jesus and his meaning include the Johannine approaches to people of faith who come to believe in Jesus.

Please read: John 1.1-18

The gospel begins with a hymn to the Word of God. The author chose a title, "Word," widely used in Jewish and Hellenistic (Greek philosophical) circles and used it as an instrument to set forth the meaning of Jesus. Jesus not only speaks the word of God, Jesus *is* the Word of God. The Synoptics record the astonishment of the listeners of Jesus; John gives the reason: Jesus's words are the Word of the Father who sent him. He speaks only what he has heard from the Father (Jn 8.40; 14.24). The identity between the word of Jesus and the word of the Father is not due to inspiration as was true for the prophets but derives from the presence of the Word with the Father before the Incarnation. This makes Jesus the unique revelation of the Father.

Throughout the Gospel of John the word refers to the person of Jesus and designates the revelation of Jesus himself and his sonship. The use of "Word" in the prologue signifies the ultimate state of evolution of the use of this title. The development moves from an appreciation of Jesus speaking the word of God to an identification between Jesus and the Word of God and finally to a title applied to Jesus.

We might then ask why the title is not used in the rest of the gospel but found only in the prologue? The intention of the evangelist seems to have been to identify the Word of God with the Word made flesh and once this identification was made, he may freely move away from the title and concentrate on the Word made flesh.

When we read the prologue we immediately become aware of the pre-existence of the Word and the implications for the divinity of Jesus. This captures part of the teaching of the gospel but not all, for John always has in mind the Word become flesh. The Word in the prologue becomes the words in the mouth of Jesus and finally Jesus himself to whom the disciples must respond in faith if they are to accept the revelation of the Father that Jesus offers. If the divinity is the root of the revelation of Jesus, the humanity reflects this revelation.

THE SON OF MAN

Please read: John 1. 51; 3. 13-14; 5. 27; 6. 27, 52-53, 62; 8. 28; 9. 35; 12. 23, 34; 13. 31

This title Son of Man is common to all the gospels but the author of John used the title in a distinctive way. The author of the Fourth Gospel accepts the Synoptic tradition of the Son of Man as Judge to come as well as the aspect of the suffering Son of Man but he deepens the concept and modifies the title to bring out the pre-existence as well as the elevation and glorification of Jesus.

The careful reading of the above texts brings to the forefront the centrality of the Johannine notion of pre-existence. The possibility of exaltation, the simultaneous judgment of the world and the entire mission of the one who came to give life has its origins in the heavenly pre-existence. The only explanation of 3.13 and 6.62 is the pre-supposition that in the Son of Man God has already set his seal (6.27) and from him the Son has received a transcendent message (3.11-13) and this in turn is the guarantee of his future return (6.62). The Son of Man has a privileged relationship with God.

An additional element in the understanding of the meaning of the Son of Man has similarities with what we have seen in regard to the Word. While the title does emphasize the pre-existence and the divinity of Jesus, like the title Word, it also connotes a human aspect.

15

The Fourth Gospel is well known for its words with more than one level of meaning. Recent studies show that the title Son of Man can also mean just "man" or "everyman" or "anyone." Possibly the author of the Fourth Gospel also had this meaning in mind. The title would then imply an emphasis on the human. The author seems fond of using "man" even when an elliptical expression would serve, e.g., in 5.12 his use of "man" for Jesus is striking. What John seems to be implying is the divinity present within a true humanity. Faithfully, the gospel narrates the weariness of Jesus at the well (Jn 4.6), his sorrow and pain over Lazarus (11.33). It also speaks of Jesus as the son of Joseph (6.42; 1.45). As much as power is stressed in the gospel it is not an independent power. The signs Jesus works are in answer to prayer (11.41); of himself he can do nothing. His works are those which the Father gives him. And yet this man is *the man,* the ideal person in the sense that he is what we should be and is the means of attaining personhood for all. The insistence on Jesus' real humanity and the teaching on love in the Fourth Gospel (15. 12) are complementary safeguards against the idea that Jesus is an abstract or docetic Christ. The historical and the eternal, the human and the divine combine in the title Son of Man.

THE SON OF GOD, THE SON

Please read: John 1.49; 5.22; 10.36; 19.7; 20.31

The Fourth Gospel, like the Synoptics, uses the title "Son of God" as well as "Son." The former does not appear frequently but when it does, the author uses it forcefully. John 20.31, the original conclusion of the gospel, shows us that the purpose of the book was to help hearers to believe that Jesus is the Lord, the Son of God. John also uses this title in his opening chapter (1.49) and at the trial before Pilate (19.7).

These and the other above-mentioned passages show that the title Son of God points to Jesus as the one sent by the Father. But this does not sufficiently specify the relationship between Jesus as the Son, and God as the Father. The use of "Son" characterizes the special relationship between God and Jesus.

Please read: John 3.17, 35; 5.20, 22

The title designates first of all Jesus' close relationship to God. As a result of this relationship, the Son does nothing of himself but only what he sees the Father doing. The author seems to present a picture of the Son who is dependent upon the Father for everything and one who is joined to the Father through love and obedience.

Please read: John 5.21; 8.36; 3.36; 6.40; 5.22

Other texts imply equality. The Son gives life as does the Father (5.21). The Son makes us free (8.36); the Son also gives eternal life (3.36; 6.40). The Father has also given all judgment to the Son (5.22). As we examine these texts the Son seems to stand in equality with the Father as a divine being, and cannot be easily distinguished from God. The gospel does identify the Son with God (in the prologue, 1.1, the Word is identified with God, "And the Word was God," and in 20.28, Thomas refers to Jesus as "my Lord and my God," but both instances have additional problems associated with them which prevent a completely unequivocal identification. Surely, however, these examples imply a high christology in the early Church which thought of Jesus as equal to God. The question then arises: Is the Son in reality God descending into the human sphere and becoming manifest so that the divine being is unveiled in the lowliness of Jesus of Nazareth?

Please read: John 3. 31-35; 5.19, 20; 8. 54;
10. 36; 14. 28; 17. 3

17

In traditional piety many quickly identified Jesus with God. Such a conclusion must take into consideration, however, other passages which imply something different. The Jesus of the Fourth Gospel proclaims that the Father is greater than he is (14. 28) and speaks of the Father as the only true God (17.3). The Father has glorified the Son (8.54) and consecrated him and sent him into the world (10.36). The Son speaks and acts dependently upon the Father (3. 31-35; 15.15).

THE SON AS HUMAN

> *Please read: John 2. 1-14; 4.7, 31; 6. 42;*
> *7. 3, 5, 8, 10, 27; 8. 40; 10. 33; 11. 5-33.*

The author of this gospel emphasizes the humanity of Jesus as well as his divinity. He hungers and thirsts (4. 7, 31); he weeps and becomes angry (2. 14; 4. 6; 11. 33); he loves Lazarus and his sisters (11. 5); and he seems to change his mind (7. 8, 10). Jesus accuses his enemies of seeking to kill him because he speaks of what he has heard from God (8.40) but the Jews reply that they seek to kill him because he is a man and makes himself equal to God (5. 18; 10. 33; 19. 7). He also came from Nazareth. Jesus is an earthly man without exception. Nor does he even hint that the origin of Jesus was other than from an earthly father and mother as do Luke and Matthew. He is of the earth and also divine.

John has located the man Jesus so close to God that down to the present time the opinion prevailed that the Johannine theology of glory no longer took seriously the humanity of Jesus. Some foundation exists for this opinion but upon closer examination of the gospel such an opinion contradicts the evangelist's recognized intention. John wished to give expression to the Christian belief that God had spoken perfectly and finally in the Man Jesus. The emphasis on the divinity may tend at times to eclipse or obscure the humanity but a closer reading of the texts shows that John strove

18

to avoid such conclusions. Jesus is the Son, pre-existent and divine, united with God who is Father, sent into the world as man and as man he reveals the Father as the one who sent him.

THE USE OF "I AM"

Please read: John 4. 26; 6. 20; 8. 24, 28, 58;
13. 19; 18. 5, 6, 8

The use of "I am" in the Fouth Gospel is unusual. Nine times the author uses it as a title in an absolute sense. In each of these instances Jesus is the speaker and he addresses a variety of audiences: disciples who are friendly, some who are opposed to him and finally some who are instrumental in his death.

The expression can mean "I am the one," as is evident in John 9. 9, but it means much more. A study of a similar use of the expression in Isaiah 40–55 shows that the expression is always used by Yahweh and signifies that Yahweh alone is God. John selected this terminology to indicate the relationship between Jesus and God as well as to inaugurate a new age accomplished by his presence.

A good example of the subtlety is found in chapter 18. When his captors draw near and Jesus questions them on whom they seek, they reply, "Jesus the Nazorean." Jesus answers, "I am he," and quite appropriately in the presence of the divine, "they retreated slightly and fell to the ground."

With this title the author expresses the unity that exists between Jesus and his Father. John clearly teaches the divinity of Jesus, his oneness with the Father, in his choice of the phrase, "I am." At the same time we still have a possible double meaning since the expression can also mean "I am the one." The divine being is present in the historical dimension of space and time. Once again the theological and the historical are united as is time and eternity.

"I AM" WITH EXPRESSED PREDICATE

Please read: John 1. 20; 3. 38; 6. 35, 41, 48, 51;
8. 12, 18; 10, 7, 9, 11, 14; 11. 25; 14. 6; 15. 1, 5

Together with the use of "I am" in an absolute sense the Gospel of John also uses the expression with various predicates: light, bread of life, shepherd, vine, way, truth, the resurrection, door, etc. The author chooses an expression that can relate Jesus to divinity and then uses that same expression to talk about what is essential for human life: bread, drink, guidance, direction. Salvation is actualized in the personal activity of Jesus for the sake of others. Once again we deal with two levels of meaning and interpretation. The absolute use of "I am" emphasized the divinity of Jesus and his close relationship to God the Father. The use of "I am" with a predicate unites Jesus to the one who brings salvation personally and in a way that is experienced as part of and essential to human life. The divine and human co-exist in the one Jesus of Nazareth.

THE CHRIST (MESSIAH)

Please read: John 1. 17, 41; 4. 25, 29; 7. 26, 27,
31, 41, 42; 9. 22; 11. 27; 12. 34; 17. 3; 20. 31

Jewish thought about the messiah emphasized a divinely anointed and endowed son of David who would restore the glory of Israel and destroy the hated pagan rule. The Fourth Gospel considers this inadequate and incomplete. The gospel opens with the confession that Jesus is the messiah and the established purpose in chapter 20 is to show listeners that Jesus was in truth the messiah, the Son of God. The meaning, however, is in direct opposition to Jewish expectations and traditions.

As messiah Jesus is king but not in a political sense (18. 36). When the people wanted to make him king, Jesus fled (6.15). For the author of this gospel the kingship of Jesus was spiritual. The messiah fulfilled Old Testament expectations through the gift of eternal life offered to believers and already part of their inheritance in faith.

The title messiah would combine the spiritual and the temporal, the divine and the human. As the incarnation of Wisdom Jesus as messiah lived in the divine realm but also in the human realm. The giver of eternal life offers this to people in history.

The presentation of Johannine christology combines the human and the divine, but also includes the human response. The historical Jesus was related to the experience in faith of the believer; the glory was manifested humanly so that the individual could respond to the veiled glory; the function of Jesus, his revelation of the Father, was the revelation of his person as one who was from the Father and going to the Father. In each instance, the christology depended on its conclusion: the individual response of the believer. The gospel is centered on christology but completed only in an analysis of individual faith.

SUGGESTIONS FOR REFLECTION

1. Jesus is the "Word" of God. What does this title mean to you and how can the "Word" help you in understanding the mission of Jesus?

2. The Son of Man emphasizes the divinity of Jesus. If it can also mean "everyman," how does this affect your understanding of the Johannine theology of Jesus' humanity and divinity?

3. Jesus is the Son. This title is more important than Son of God. If Jesus is the Son, what does that imply for your understanding of your own relationship to God?

4. The use of "I am" is unusual in this gospel. After you have studied all of the times it is used, what are your thoughts on its value for understanding Jesus? Especially relate the use without and with a predicate.

5. Jesus was never a political messiah. Would you prefer him to be understood politically today? How can he be a messiah if he is not involved with the political and social aspects of human life?

6. How do you relate the humanity and divinity of Jesus in your own life and how has this been affected by your study of the Gospel of John?

CHAPTER III

INDIVIDUALS
IN THE FOURTH GOSPEL

Faith in the Fourth Gospel is the human response to the revelation of Jesus. The acceptance is active; a decision must be made. When Jesus enters into a person's life the individual has the opportunity to lose any illusions and accept the offered salvation. The true believer accepts Jesus not just as a miracle worker but as the Son of God.

In this process the Father plays a significant role. No movement to faith is possible without the presence of the Father. The Father gives the disciples to Jesus and actually teaches them through Jesus. We must now turn to these individual believers and learn just how the author uses them as representative figures. The author chose various persons from the common gospel tradition or selected them from his own tradition to illustrate some point about the nature of faith, its presence or its lack. These individuals are not merely figments of the writer's imagination; nor are they described in a completely historical way. Rather they have a historical foundation but are presented in a peculiarly Johannine way to teach the evangelist's readers or audience something about the faith in Jesus that gives life.

JOHN THE BAPTIST

Please read: John 1.19-34; 3. 22-30; 1. 6-8, 15;
4.1-3; 5.33-36; 10.40-42

The introductory narrative about John the Baptist (1. 19-34) is followed by another scene in which John appears (3.22-30). Two rather problematic sections (1.6-8, 15 and 4.1-3) may be the work of an editor who inserted these to counteract the influence of John on some contemporaries of the editor. In two other passages Jesus speaks of John (5.33-36; 10.40-42). The Johannine John the Baptizer differs considerably from the John presented in the Synoptics. To begin with we refer to him as the "Baptizer" in the Synoptics. In the Fourth Gospel he is never so designated. He is simply John. Surely the readers knew that John baptized but the activity is not introduced until verse 25.

The John of the Fourth Gospel is a John of Christian faith. He has come to bear testimony to the light; he has accepted Jesus and then becomes his witness. He confesses that Jesus is the lamb of God (1.29) and he on whom the Spirit remains (1.32). His representative role is stated in the verse which stands as the climax of the first great pericope on the Baptist: "I have seen for myself and have testified, 'This is God's chosen One' " (1.34).

John is an individual come from God and sent from God who has recognized the presence of the Spirit in Jesus and has confessed that Jesus is the Son of God. We need not emphasize his role in baptizing. He is the first example of the fulfillment of Johannine christology in a confessing believer.

24

NATHANAEL

Please read: John 1.43-51; 21.2

Nathanael appears only in the Johannine tradition. We hear of him first in the call of the first disciples and he reappears in the final chapter with the other disciples as they go fishing. His first appearance can be viewed as a transformed vocation scene. The conversation between Jesus and Nathanael seems contrived to lead to the great testimony: "You are the Son of God; you are the king of Israel" (1.49).

This disciple represents the true Israelite who comes to faith in Jesus. The author describes him as a man seated "under the fig tree." To a perceptive reader this recalls the Jewish tradition about the study of the scriptures under the fig tree. Jesus reveals God and perceives the incipient faith in a man who bears an Old Testament name and engages in activity most characteristic of God's people and actually uses a technical formula for revelation identifying him as an "Israelite. There is no guile in him" (1.47).

Nathanael responds with a profession of personal faith and calls Jesus the "king of Israel," a traditional messianic title (Mk 15.32). To this confession John adds the additional confession, "Son of God." This additional title brings the confession in accord with the christology of the gospel which sees Jesus as the messiah because he is God's Son, not in the Old Testament sense of one specially chosen, but in the typically Johannine sense of the one who has a unique relationship with God the Father.

Nathanael had searched the scriptures and had come to
believe in Jesus and made his personal commitment to him.
He has no need to ask Jesus: "Who are you?" Nathanael
will learn who Jesus is but because Jesus has called him
the true Israelite, he receives the answer to his unasked
question: Jesus is the Son of Man (1.51). This verse may
have been added to the Nathanael episode at a later stage
of the development of the gospel tradition. Its presence
contributes to the theology of the gospel not only because
of the meaning of the title "Son of Man" which we have
already studied, but because the title makes Nathanael the
first bearer of a formula which presents Jesus as both the
Son of God and Son of Man. Nathanael has responded
most personally to the revelation of Jesus as both titles
imply.

NICODEMUS

Please read: John 3.1-15; 19.38-42

The episode of Nicodemus coming to Jesus at night exemplifies an imperfect coming to faith. He is impressed by
Jesus and calls him Master (3.2). He apparently belongs
to a group of people drawn to Jesus because of his miracles
but also as one who goes beyond the mere miraculous: "No
man can perform signs and wonders such as you perform
unless God is with him" (3.2). This faith, however, remains
insufficient. Nicodemus may represent people of good will
who also may be leaders of the people but have difficulties
in accepting Jesus. The forebodings of Jesus in verses 11
and 12 cannot be forgotten: the individual may come to
Jesus impressed by signs but must be drawn by the Father
to Jesus in order to accept him in faith.

Scholars disagree on many aspects of this dialogue. Of
particular note is the discussion on the discourse of Jesus.
Is it from Jesus or is it a kerygmatic speech by the evan-

gelist, or the Beloved Disciple? Also, where does the dialogue between Jesus and Nicodemus end, and is the discourse then continued by Jesus, by the teaching of the Beloved Disciple, or by the evangelist? Some hold for a break after verse 12 with the rest a kerygmatic discourse by the evangelist. Some see the break after verse 16.

For our purposes we can hold that the entire discourse is a condensation of the principle assertions of Johannine theology and therefore comes from the teaching of the Beloved Disciple. Jesus, having been sent by the Father, reveals the Father. Jesus accomplishes this full revelation and redemption on the cross. On the part of the individual, Jesus offers a summons that demands a personal decision actually accomplished through the power of God.

Perhaps the original episode between Jesus and Nicodemus was part of the original sign source but this gave rise to a fuller theology of coming to faith in Jesus. The break in verse 12 or 16 can be the seam from the original source.

The further question of the identity of the speaker remains unsolved. Possibly the author joins some legitimate remembrances of Jesus' teaching to an historical episode but we need not insist that the teaching is tied irrevocably to an encounter with Nicodemus. The theological meaning remains primary: the difficulties experienced by an individual who accepts Jesus in some way, but who needs the powerful assistance of God, in order to come to faith in Jesus.

THE SAMARITAN WOMAN

Please read: John 4.1-42

The coming to faith by the Samaritan woman and her profession of Jesus as the messiah contrasts sharply with the searchers of miracles in John 2.23-25, the bewilderment of Nicodemus in John 3.1-12, and even the suspicious attitude of the Pharisees in John 4.13. Jesus gives living water, reveals true worship, and offers salvation. The woman comes to Jesus, responds openly to his invitation, and ultimately believes in him.

Commentators do not agree on the historicity of the narrative. Like the previous study of Nicodemus, we are dealing with a narrative composed by the evangelist with probably some historical foundation. Many aspects of the chapter show points of contact with Old Testament themes as well as rabbinic tradition. Whatever the origin of the narrative the author focuses on the encounter between Jesus and the woman.

A study of the development of the themes involved highlights the relationship between Jesus and the woman:
verses 7-10: the first exchange introduces the topic of living water and challenges the woman.
verses 11-15: the woman misunderstands and Jesus clarifies that he is speaking of the water of eternal life to which the woman responds by requesting this water. Still, the woman has yet to recognize Jesus.
verses 16-18: Jesus takes the initiative by speaking of her personal life leading her to recognize who he is.
verses 19-26: the woman recognizes that Jesus is a prophet and turns away from her personal life to ask about worship. Jesus explains that true worship can come only from those begotten by the Spirit. Finally, the woman recognizes Jesus as the messiah and affirms her conclusions by becoming a missionary to her townsfolk.

The episode narrates a gradual unfolding of the self-revelation of Jesus, with all of the Johannine themes involved: revelation, the need for a personal decision of faith, the influence of the power of God, messianic titles, various levels of meaning. The conclusion of the episode includes the reaction of the townspeople as well: they too come to faith not on the word of the woman but through their own experience of Jesus.

The chapter also presents the familiar christological theme of the author which unites the revelation of Jesus to the faith of the individual. The use of "I am," the messiah, and the implications of "Father"—all point to the fundamental christology previously studied.

THE ROYAL OFFICIAL

> *Please read: John 4. 46-53; Matthew 8.5-13;*
> *Luke 7.1-10*

Contemporary commentators who hold for a sign source for this gospel assign this encounter between Jesus and the royal official to this pre-Johannine material. Additional considerations surround this pericope. The Johannine material agrees in many details with the cure of the official's son described in Matthew 8.5-13 and Luke 7.1-10. All three narrate the same event even though the approaches differ considerably.

John indicates the function of the official in verse 50: "The man put his trust in the word Jesus spoke to him, and started for home." As the faith of the centurion of Matthew and Luke occasioned the cure of the son, so the faith of the royal official in the word of Jesus occasioned the miracle narrated here. The Johannine narrative, however, is not as explicit about the faith of the official as is Matthew. Further differences become evident as we continue the comparison. According to John the word which the Johannine Jesus speaks gives life. The word of Jesus in the Fourth Gospel does not simply heal, but gives life. The royal official believed in the word of the Lord which brought life. The faith results from coming to Jesus in a receptive way, listening to his word and finally accepting

this word which then gives life. The Johannine Jesus
speaks and vivifies.

THE LAME MAN AND THE MAN BORN BLIND

Please read: John 5.1-18; 9.1-41

The stories of the lame man in chapter 5 and of the blind
man in chapter 9 have a similar construction. Each begins
with a miracle and each leads to a controversy between Jesus
and the Jews. The author loosely links the controversy to
the miracle story by mentioning that it occurred on the
Sabbath. Both narratives also reflect the controversy between church and synagogue at the time of the gospel and
not at the time of Jesus.

The lame man does not at first know Jesus's identity (5. 13)
and thus Jesus seeks him out a second time offering at least
a second opportunity for faith after the cure. But the man
does not make a profession of faith. He has experienced the
healing power of Jesus and now faces a moment critical for
faith. Unfortunately he remains content with the cure and
does not come to faith. Jesus offered the opportunity but
the man refused.

The blind man, on the contrary, exemplifies an occasion
when the sign led to faith. The author constructs his narrative to emphasize the hardening of the nonbelieving Jew
in the presence of the revelation of Jesus and the gradual
unfolding of faith on the part of the receptive blindman.
He confesses that Jesus is a prophet (9.17); a man from
God (9. 33); and finally, he believes in him as the Son of
Man (9. 37). The sick, sinful blind man becomes the healthy
good man who sees; those who appear good and healthy and
can see, turn out to be bad and unhealthy and blind.

This story also contains some of the chief theological themes
in the gospel. Jesus does the works of his Father (9. 4); he

is light and offers the same to people (9. 5); and in the final section Jesus reveals himself as the Son of Man (9. 35). Within the dialogue Jesus is called a prophet (9. 17) and a man from God (9. 33); and an oblique reference to Jesus as messiah occurs in the explanation of the fear of the parents (9. 22).

Jesus manifests himself and gradually the blind man "sees" and believes in him. Unlike the lame man, the blind man does not stop at the cure but believes in Jesus as the Son of Man. The author contrasts the profession of personal acceptance of Jesus by the blind man with the Pharisees' refusal to accept him. The revelation reaches out to the individual believer and invites a positive response freely offered and freely accepted.

PHILIP

Please read: John 1. 43-51; 6. 1-15; 12. 20-36; 14. 1-14.

Philip is a mystery in this gospel. Four times he appears (1. 43-51; 6. 1-15; 12. 20-36; 14. 1-14). The meaning of the latter three appearances depends on the interpretation of the first appearance. In the first chapter Philip appears as a believing disciple. He heard the call of Jesus and accepted him as "the one Moses spoke of in the law—the prophets too" (1. 45). In this episode, however, Nathanael overshadows Philip. He comes into his own only when we also compare the other places in the gospel where we find him mentioned.

In the sixth chapter Philip is portrayed as a believer, but his understanding was partial and he needed the further direction of Jesus (6.6).

Philip holds a similar role in chapter 14. He does not fully know Jesus; he has not understood the revelation which Jesus offered. He made his commitment to Jesus but he did

31

not fully appreciate the christology that underlay the coming of Jesus. Philip sought a theophany such as Moses or Aaron or the elders of Israel had experienced. But no such theophany was given. Jesus revealed God but in the human way, expressed in his ordinary human life.

The final episode casts Philip in still another role. The Greeks wish to see Jesus and ask Philip who tells Andrew. Both disciples bear Greek names and Philip was identified as coming from Galilee (1. 44). The symbolism is complete. Just as the Samaritans met Jesus through the testimony of a Samaritan (4. 28), so the Greeks meet Jesus through one who represents the "Greek disciples."

Philip represents the misunderstanding or the lack of complete understanding on the part of those who believe. He also represents those who act as missionaries for others. The christology of John manifests the need for completion in faith and also admits the possibility of some misunderstanding which cannot destroy the fundamental faith.

MARTHA AND MARY

Please read: John 11. 1-44

Throughout the chapter dealing with the raising of Lazarus Martha believes in Jesus but unlike the Samaritan woman, Martha's faith seems incomplete. In verse 27 she addresses Jesus with lofty titles, probably used in the early profession of faith by believers, but in verse 39 she shows that she has yet to believe in his power. Martha sees Jesus an an intermediary between God and people (11. 22) but she does not understand that Jesus also gives life (11. 25). Jesus then acts out a drama of the gift of life by raising Lazarus which proves to Martha that he has power to give life in the present and not just in the future. Jesus does not reject her traditional understanding of faith and the titles that she chose to use, but himself chose to demonstrate the deeper truth that lay behind them. Martha found it difficult to believe that Jesus brings life into this present world. Jesus gives her a dramatic assurance.

Mary meets Jesus in the same chapter and falls at his feet but like Martha does not display a particularly deep faith. Both display a faith in carefully chosen words but neither seems to understand its meaning. Jesus raises Lazarus to attest to the future resurrection for all of those who will believe in him now. Jesus comes into this world as the messiah (11. 27), the Son of God who gives life to all who come and believe in him.

The christological manifestation in this chapter once again joins the profession of faith as an integrating element. Jesus verifies this faith by the actual raising of Lazarus. He then promises to give life to all who believe in him, and the raising of Lazarus is a proof of the reality of his statement. Jesus possesses a power to save all who will accept him as one whom the Father has sent into the world.

JUDAS

Please read: John 6. 67-71; 12. 1-8; 13. 2, 26-30;
18. 2-5

Judas appears as one of the Twelve (6. 67-71); at the account of the anointing of Jesus (12. 1-8); in the supper scene (13. 26-30); in the passion account (18. 2-5). Each appearance has a parallel in the Synoptics but each also has a particular Johannine characteristic. The evangelist borrowed from the general tradition that Judas was the betrayer but added to this basic element further insights about him. He was a thief who took what was not his own; he was a figure of the night and more specifically, the one into whom the devil entered (13.2). Judas allied himself with the chief priests and Pharisees (18.3). He was the supreme example of one to whom faith was offered but rejected.

In the opening scene of the passion Jesus asked the question: "Who is it you want?" (18. 4). This question can be viewed as the christological question par excellence. In the Fourth Gospel the answer unfolds gradually. Jesus responds: "I am" (18. 5, 6, 8). The use of this expression, as we have seen, evokes awe and adoration. The formula reveals Jesus. Judas stands by as he had been present in the ministry of Jesus. Jesus offered him the possibility of faith; he could walk in the light but chose to stay in the darkness and turn away from Jesus to himself. The moment of the passion brings two worlds into conflict: that of the Father of whom the person of Jesus is the supreme revelation and that of darkness and evil and unbelief, represented by Judas. Jesus confronts Judas but Judas turns away to the darkness and refuses to believe.

MARY

Please read: John 2. 1-11; 6. 42; 19. 25-27

A study of individuals in this gospel must include the Mother of the Lord even if it may create more questions than can be adequately treated here. Mary appears at Cana (2. 1-11) and at the foot of the cross (19. 25-27). The crowds make mention of her in John 6. 42 when they are divided as to the meaning of the activity of Jesus and remark: "Is this not Jesus, the son of Joseph? Do we not know his father and mother?" Mary is not called by her given name but called: "the mother of Jesus" or "his mother"; she makes no formal profession of faith in her Son and when Jesus speaks to her, he calls her "woman."

The Fathers of the Church interpreted the figure of Mary in this gospel symbolically and the trend continues today. Mary lives as an example of firm faith. Her faith in her son forms the foundation for her role in both instances in this gospel.

Mary believed in him and with her faith, patiently awaited the fulfillment of that faith. She joins the Beloved Disciple at Calvary in a common faith and a common expectation for the full revelation that took place in the "Hour" of Jesus.

Mary in the gospel does not represent someone coming to faith but the one who has already believed and who remains steadfast in that faith. She does not need explanations for her faith, nor do we have any reference to the origin of her faith. The author used this model believer to teach another aspect of faith demanded and expected by Jesus. If we have seen Philip as an example of a lack of full understanding, Mary demonstrates the need for fidelity and the reward for fidelity even when there can be no full understanding.

MARY MAGDALENE

Please read: John 20. 1-2, 11-18

Mary Magdalene appears twice in chapter 20. The second appearance dramatically presents the faith response of Mary to the risen Lord. The former can be seen as a Johannine redaction of the visit of the women to the tomb to single out the figure of Mary Magdalene and de-emphasize the Easter events in favor of Calvary. This decision to emphasize Mary Magdalene falls well within the tendency of the gospel to highlight an individual.

The episode may contain an apologetic overtone. The objection that the disciples have stolen the body cannot be valid because the possibility of grave-robbing was already raised by one of Jesus's followers. The apologetic, however, does not constitute the main purpose of the narrative. Mary believes in the risen Lord. Jesus revealed himself directly by calling her name and she responded by calling him "Teacher" (20. 26), as did the first two disciples and Nicodemus (1. 38; 3. 3). Mary does not at first understand the meaning of the resurrection and tries to hold on to Jesus (20. 17). Jesus him-

35

self must interpret the resurrection for her: the risen Lord must ascend to the Father. Jesus did not return to life through resuscitation. After Mary realized the meaning of the resurrection she became a true believer for she announced: "I have seen the Lord" (20. 18). Mary became a believer in the ascending Lord only because Jesus himself revealed his resurrection. The Gospel of John used the example of Mary Magdalene to enhance the depth of faith expected of an individual: before he was accepted as one who revealed the Father; now after his resurrection Jesus must be believed as the one who has returned to the Father.

THOMAS

Please read: John 11. 16; 14. 5; 20. 24-29

In the same chapter which contains the dramatic scene with Mary Magdalene the author of the Fourth Gospel has composed another dramatic scene between Jesus and Thomas. Earlier the author had mentioned Thomas as a leader among the disciples (11. 16). His appearance here links the resurrection of Lazarus with the death of Jesus.

Thomas appears again in chapter 14 exemplifying ignorance: "Lord, we do not know where you are going. How can we know the way?" Even before we meet him in chapter 20 Thomas epitomizes the bravado and the ignorance of the disciples.

The principal point in chapter 20 is the resurrection of Jesus. Jesus invites Thomas to believe in him because Thomas has experienced him as risen. In some ways, the doubting Thomas is incidental to the main point of the narrative. The reality of the resurrection and Thomas's belief in Jesus as risen forms the central meaning of the narrative. This sets the stage for the profession of faith in verse 29. Thomas explicitly confesses belief in the divinity of Jesus, the crucified one who is risen and who is his Lord and God. The final saying by Jesus emphasizes the later situation of the community: individuals believe as Thomas did but without the appearance of the risen Lord. Even the profession of faith by Thomas may come from the attempt of the later Christian community to join together a belief in the humanity and divinity of Jesus.

PETER

Please read: John 1. 41; 6. 8, 68; 13. 6, 9, 24, 36; 18. 10; 15. 25; 20. 2, 4, 6; 21. 2-15

Simon Peter figures prominently in all of the gospels. The characterization of Peter in the Fourth Gospel, however, raises the question of the importance of Peter to the Johannine Church and his relationship to the Beloved Disciple. His role in the final chapter recalls more his image in the Synoptics especially the Matthean passage on the keys of the kingdom (Mt 16. 13-20). This final chapter, as we have mentioned, comes from a hand later than that of the evangelist. When Peter appears in other places in the gospel he is related to the Beloved Disciple, with the author creating almost a rivalry and competition.

The sequences in the gospel wherein Peter appears often show some evidence of contact with the Synoptic tradition. These same passages, however, still manifest a peculiar approach by the evangelist placing Peter in a subordinate role to the Beloved Disciple.

Peter appears first in John 1. 40-42. The author of the gospel joins in this one passage the call of Simon in the Synoptics to the imposition of a symbolic name (Mk 1. 16-18; Mt 4. 18-20; Lk 5. 1-11; and Mk 3. 16; Mt 16.17; Lk 6. 14). Jesus acts in this gospel from the outset as the divine Jesus demanding faith and seeing into a person sufficiently to change his name. Peter with his new name joins the disciples, having been led to Jesus through the testimony of his brother Andrew.

The second Johannine passage with some contact with the Synoptics occurs in the confession of Peter in chapter 6. The mention of the Twelve (the first of the two references in the gospel) also shows the traditional nature of the episode. The profession of faith by Peter, however, differs radically from that of the Synoptics. Peter speaks for the disciples who have come to explicit faith that Jesus reveals the words of eternal life: "You have the words of eternal life. We have come to believe; we are convinced that you are God's holy one (6. 68-69). The Synoptics record Peter's confession of Jesus as messiah. The Fourth Gospel bases the messiahship of Jesus on his mission to reveal. The confession concentrates on the role of revealing.

The third passage (20. 3-10) contrasts Peter with the Beloved Disciple. Both run to the tomb; the Beloved Disciple arrives first, allows Peter to enter, but Peter does not come to faith in the risen Lord although the Beloved Disciple "saw and believed" (20. 8).

The appendix to the gospel adds a further description of Peter. The final editor probably desired to present Peter in a way more consistent with the common understanding of Peter at the end of the first century. He lists Peter first among the disciples (21. 2); describes him as a fisherman (21. 3, 11) and presents him as one who has seen and recognized the risen Lord (21. 14). The juxtaposition with the Beloved Disciple remains but the focus centers on the leader of the disciples and his pastoral office. Peter passed his test of love after he had failed his test of fidelity. Once he has professed a belief and a love of the Lord he can assume his responsibilities as the leader of the disciples. Earlier Peter had believed in the revealer and spoke for the disciples; here he assumes a close relationship with Jesus through personal choice and accepts a care for the sheep.

THE BELOVED DISCIPLE

Please read: John 13. 21-26; 18. 15-16;
19. 25-27; 20. 2-10; 21. 2-24

The Beloved Disciple remains an enigmatic figure. In the final chapter he appears in two scenes alongside Peter; he rests his head on the breast of Jesus at the Last Supper, stands with the Mother of Jesus at the foot of the cross, and runs with Peter to the tomb on Easter morn. In the latter scene the author also calls him "the other disciple" and for this reason we can identify the other disciple in chapter 18 with the Beloved Disciple.

Over the course of the centuries many have attempted to identify him with John the son of Zebedee, or with Lazarus, John Mark, or John the presbyter known to Papias and Polycarp (see Acts 12.25). No satisfactory solution to his identity has even been found. Since the evangelist chose to shroud him in anonymity, we probably should refrain from trying to discover his identity and study rather his position in the gospel.

The Beloved Disciple in this gospel is not just one among many followers of the Lord. He epitomizes the believer, the disciple, the beloved and the witness to Jesus. As a believer the author contrasts him with Peter. Both run to the tomb but only the Beloved Disciple believes. The same is true in the comparison with Mary Magdalene. She does not come to faith in seeing the empty tomb. For him the empty tomb suffices. His conduct illustrates the saying of Jesus in chapter 20: "Blest are they who have not seen and have believed." Nor does his faith rest on the testimony of the scriptures: "as yet they did not understand the Scripture that Jesus had to rise from the dead" (20. 9). The Beloved Disciple believes firmly and fully. In the final chapter the editor continues this tradition by having the Beloved Disciple proclaim to Peter: "It is the Lord" (21.7).

The author calls him a disciple. He followed after Jesus and believed in his word. Discipleship in this gospel extends beyond the narrow group known as the Twelve. Since the Twelve do not figure prominently in the gospel, we need not identify him with one of the Twelve. Perhaps he was a resident of Jerusalem who came to know Jesus only in his final ministry. He may not have followed him for the entire period of preaching but possessed the hallmark of all true disciples of Jesus: belief in him and a love of the brethren.

The author also describes him as the one whom Jesus loved (Jn 13. 23; 19. 26; 20. 2; 21. 7, 10). He shared an intimacy with Jesus at the Last Supper and also a community of faith with the Mother of Jesus on Calvary.

Because the Beloved Disciple related to Jesus so closely, he could give witness and testimony. This bond of intimacy qualifies the Disciple to lead others to believe and have eternal life. He witnessed to the death of Jesus (Jn 19.35), and in the conclusion of the gospel, the final editor lays his testimony before the contemporary reader in the form of the Johannine gospel.

The Beloved Disciple exemplifies all that faith in Jesus implies. He shows the witness of John the Baptizer, the steadfast faith of Mary the Mother of Jesus, the acceptance of Nathanael, as well as the faith of the man born blind, of Peter, Mary Magdalene, and Thomas. The very complex Johannine christology which demanded a full belief in Jesus as the revealer of God, his human face, finds fulfillment in the Beloved Disciple.

The analysis of individuals in the Fourth Gospel underlines the close relationship between Jesus and his followers. Johannine christology moves outward to a personal acceptance by the individual believer. In each of the representative figures studied, the author singled out some aspect of faith for our consideration. We have seen the growth of faith, the motives for faith, the role of the Father in bringing people to faith and the content of faith: Jesus and his mission. The various people who populate this gospel offer a variety of approaches to Jesus and help the contemporary reader to appreciate the differences still present in the Christian community. The people are representative figures: they exhibit more than just their historical relationship to the Lord. They stand eternally as symbols of others who struggle with the age old question of faith in the Lord Jesus.

SUGGESTIONS FOR REFLECTION

1. The study of individuals in the gospel can be fascinating. How have you been affected by the various characters? Do you relate more to some than to others?

2. Compare Nicodemus and the Samaritan woman. Examine in particular their personalities as portrayed in the gospel. How would you relate to them as individuals?

3. Mary is a firm believer. From your appreciation of Mary in your religious education, compare her with the image in this gospel. What makes her so attractive?

4. The Beloved Disciple is the ideal believer. Do you think of him as an historical person or not? Is he too good to be true? What value does he have for the contemporary believer?

5. Pick one of the other individuals, or several of them and compare them with Mary and the Beloved Disciple. How can the presence of so many people advance the meaning of faith in the Church?

6. Faith is primary in this gospel. How can the study of individuals help in understanding faith? What is involved in faith in Jesus? How much commitment is required?

7. The christology of John concludes in the acceptance in faith. How does this affect the teaching of Jesus in the Church?

CHAPTER IV

THE COMMUNITY BEHIND
THE FOURTH GOSPEL

Recent work on the Gospel of John has demonstrated that
the community behind the Fourth Gospel was not part of
the general mainstream Christianity that had developed by
the end of the first century. The Johannine tradition comes
to us from a group of people who are united in faith in the
Lord and joined by a bond of mutual love.

Previously in this work we have mentioned the possibility of
the community being founded by the Beloved Disciple, an
eyewitness but not one of the Twelve. To him the community was indebted for its particular approach to Christian
faith. Throughout the gospel the indebtedness to this early
eyewitness can be detected, especially when the community
seems to be taking a different position from that of the then-
developing Churches. To understand the community behind
the Fourth Gospel demands a closer analysis of implicit and
explicit signs of the community. Later in this work we shall
deal with sacraments in the Gospel of John which are explicit signs of the community and we shall study the conferral of pastoral office on Peter in the final chapter. In this
section I would like to examine two chapters, two parables
that express the self-understanding of the Johannine community: chapter 10 with the Good Shepherd and chapter 15,
the vine and the branches.

THE GOOD SHEPHERD

Please read: John 10. 1-18

The image of the shepherd and flock is common in the Near East; it is found in the Synoptics and in the Old Testament. What distinguishes the use of the image in the Gospel of John is the reciprocal relationship between Jesus and the individual sheep. Jesus alone creates the unity of the sheepfold. Jesus relates to the individual sheep and the ground of this union rests upon the union that exists between Jesus and God. The second parable, the shepherd and the sheep, rather than the parable of the door and the sheepfold, clarifies these points.

Jesus calls his sheep by name and they know his voice. He does not confuse them and they feel secure with the sound of his voice. Calling by name has a long biblical tradition implying knowing the person, being intimate with the person and even having power over the person. Jesus unites the individual with himself which gives security and intimacy.

The author interprets the parable in verses 14-16. Again, he expresses the intimate knowledge. In the Old Testament God knew his people intimately (Nah 1.7). Now Jesus manifests the same quality. Verse 16 stresses the purpose of this knowledge: to bring all into unity. Mutual knowledge characterizes the relationship. God knows whom he has sent and the individual sheep know whom God has sent so all know the Father and thus can have eternal life (Jn 17. 3). The author describes the unity between Father and Son as the Son being in the Father and the Father being in the Son (Jn 10. 38; 14. 11; 17. 21). He also describes this unity as "knowing" the Father (Jn 10. 15; 17. 25). Jesus knows his disciples and they know him, which implies a similar union existing between them and the Father. As the Son knows the Father and receives life from him, so those who know the Son know the Father and receive life.

44

This parable stresses the stringent bond that holds together believers with Jesus and the Father. The parable also contains implicitly the relationship among the sheep. Commentators interpret the flock in many different ways. First it seems that some of the flock in the sheepfold do not belong—only those who recognize his voice belong to Jesus. The image may be of many flocks in the one sheepfold, each belonging to a different shepherd. In the morning the different shepherds enter the fold and the sheep who belong to each will follow their shepherd out. Perhaps the larger flock stands for the Jews at the time of Jesus who did not respond to his voice.

The reference to sheep who belong to other folds could call to mind the Gentiles and their call to faith. Still further, the flock may be interpreted as a community closely related to the gnostic myth of the revealer gathering together the dispersed sparks of light trapped within each individual.

Whatever the various interpretations, the collectivity forms the foundation for the image of the individual relationship. The group exists but is diversified: some are united (those who hear his voice) and some are separated (those who do not respond). The collectivity can grow since other sheep outside this fold can be brought into it. Jesus in this parable forms the sole principle of unity based upon his union with the Father. The unity that exists among the sheep seems implicit. A personal relationship with Jesus makes possible a relationship among themselves.

The parable may mirror the historical situation of the call of Jesus to the Jews; it may also illustrate the historical situation of the troubled community being separated from the Jewish community and experiencing divisions within itself. Perhaps the author has both situations in mind, a trait not unlike other episodes in this gospel.

The precise relationship between the individual sheep remains unclear. Since the point of the chapter centered on the need to remain with Jesus as the leader and guide, we should not presume too much on the relationship between the individual sheep. Thus, if at first glance, the image of the flock appears to be an image of the Church, such a conclusion needs nuancing. The parable concerns a personal and individual relationship with Jesus, but one that presupposes the presence of a group. A group of people heard the voice of the Lord as the Good Shepherd, responded to him in faith and continued to live in the midst of those who had not responded.

THE VINE AND THE BRANCHES

Please read: John 15. 1-17

The parable of the vine and the branches should be studied along with that of the Good Shepherd. Both have a similar structure: a parable/allegory followed by an explanation. The more important relationship, however, consists in the completion of the first parable by the second. The shepherd parable stressed the individual faith response; the parable of the vine and the branches stresses the love of one another. It expands the command of love of the brethren (13. 34).

The chapter begins with a recognition formula: the identification of Jesus with the true vine and the reference to the activity of the Father. We have already noted the role of the Father in bringing people to faith in Jesus. Here the Father prunes and cuts the branches to make them more fruitful. The meaning of bearing fruit, however, does not appear until verse 12. In the opening verses of the parable the chief participants enter and we learn of their interrelationships: the Father loves Jesus and brings individuals to him; Jesus loves the Father and his disciples and the followers glorify the Father by bearing fruit, that is, by loving one another.

Unlike the parable of the shepherd, faith here is presupposed. Thus the author can emphasize love. Previously the images of living water and living bread connoted the acceptance of Jesus in faith. Here the image of the vine and the use of the words: "to live in" (ten times in verses 4-10) connotes the need for love.

The interpretation of the parable given in verses 7-17 teaches the need for love as the fulfillment of the command of Jesus. The love will be so strong that it will encourage one to give one's life for one's friend. Authentic faith must lead to such a love. Just as the Good Shepherd will lay down his life for his sheep, so each member joined to Jesus in faith will do likewise for each other. The continuation of the mission of the Lord rests upon a love for one another. The author presents a juxtaposition between the internal life of the community and its external life of mission. If the believer wishes to fulfill his or her call to discipleship, to glorify the Father, he or she will accomplish this only through an internal love of the brethren which will include the giving of one's life. The final verse culminates the discourse and makes patent the meaning of the words of Jesus.

Jesus is the whole vine and not just the stalk; he gives life to those who remain in him. Each branch receives life from Jesus and each branch must bear fruit. Some branches may even be cut off and cast into the fire. This will not affect the other branches who continue to remain with the Lord. The only possible effect, unstressed in the parable, of the loss of some branches would be the heightening of consciousness of the other branches of the need to continue to remain close to the Lord and remain steadfast in mutual love of the others. Together with Jesus the branches glorify God by loving one another.

The Good Shepherd parable stressed individual faith in Jesus with some implicit signs of a community of faith. Chapter

15 presupposed this theme and offers greater clarification by joining love to faith. The community will remain together if its members practice the love of Jesus by caring for one another. The movement from Father to Jesus to disciples concludes in the final command to love one another. Faith in Jesus not only demands the love of the Lord, but insists upon the love of the brethren.

In these chapters the basic elements of the Christian community are made evident: faith in the Lord Jesus which is personal and a love of the brethren similar to that love which Jesus himself offered to his Church. No community exists as a Christian community without faith and love. The Johannine community offered to the Christian community of all times the witness of what is fundamental for its continuance: a faith directed outside of itself to embrace the love of the other members of the community.

SUGGESTIONS FOR REFLECTION

1. The community behind the Fourth Gospel witnessed to what is fundamental. How would this affect your understanding of the Church?

2. Why would praying with other believers be essential for Christianity? Is faith of necessity a common bond?

3. Why is the one commandment of love so important in this gospel? Can you love God by loving the neighbor?

4. If the gospel seems so exclusive, how can you explain the need in Christianity for loving one's enemies? Is this gospel not concerned with members outside the community?

5. What does it mean to "live on in" Jesus?

6. Can you talk about personal faith or is it too private a matter? Can faith be a shared faith or not?

7. Is it important to know people's names? What does it mean when you know someone's name? Does Jesus know your name? What does this imply?

8. Is intimacy important for faith?

9. How does the Good Shepherd give guidance and nourishment? Who takes the place of the Good Shepherd in the Church today? Can anyone take his place?

10. Are doors important? What does a door mean and why would Jesus compare himself to a door? What do you mean when you use the word "faith"?

CHAPTER V

THE PROLOGUE:
OVERTURE FOR THE GOSPEL

A study of this nature cannot afford to examine each chapter in great detail. The purpose is to encourage the reader to continue the study of the Fourth Gospel through careful reading of the text itself and by further reading of the suggestions in the bibliography. If we study the prologue in greater detail, however, we will deal with most of the theological issues that occur repeatedly throughout the gospel.

Please read: John 1. 1-18

The prologue of the Gospel of John is a pre-existent hymn in which a later editor inserted certain verses, and then added it to the gospel. The additions can be easily detected as we move from poetry to prose. The literary structure is like a parabola: The Word in the first verse is with God, descends to become flesh in verse 14 but has returned and remains with the Father in verse 18.

When studying Johannine christology we made mention of the "Word" as a title for Jesus and its implications with regard to his pre-existence and divinity as well as the insistence by the author that this Word became flesh. The title is used only in the prologue but the verb "to speak" dominates the gospel. Jesus often speaks in this gospel and when he does, he demands attention. The content of these speeches is the work of Jesus and his relationship to the Father. (In chapters 7 and 8 the verb "to speak" is used seventeen times.

Jesus reveals himself solemnly during the feast of tabernacles).

In the gospel the disciples also listen to the word. To be a
follower of the Lord you must hear what Jesus has to say
(7. 40); you must accept his word (12. 48) and you must
remain in his word (8.31). If you believe in Jesus the word
abides within you (5.38) and this word gives spirit and life
(6. 63) but especially eternal life (12. 50).

In the past some scholars tried to show that the concept of
"Word" as contained in the prologue came from the influence of Greek philosophy. A study of ancient Greek
philosophy shows us that the "Word" was often seen as the
stable element in a world of flux, or as the primary power
or rational order in the universe which would also include
guidance for ethical behavior.

We do not have to study philosophy, however, to understand
the source for "Word" in the New Testament. In Genesis
God "said" and it was. In Isaiah 55. 10 the word is able to
effect change. In Proverbs 8. 22 Wisdom was created in the
beginning and was near to God as a confidant and a fellow
worker in creation. Jewish speculation on Wisdom gives us
enough material to understand how the author of the prologue could have composed a hymn which would be adapted
perfectly to apply to Jesus as the Word of God incarnate.

In verse 1 the words "in the beginning" may have some reference to the opening verse of Genesis. In this gospel we
have a beginning which precedes the beginning of creation.
Also in this verse the closeness of Word and God is demonstrated by the phrase "with God." The Greek preposition
connotes a nearness of persons which would never have
been used in reference to God. No one is closer to God
than the Word. Also in this verse the author refers to the
Word as God. Unfortunately our English language does not

offer us the subtlety of Greek. In Greek the word for God, *theos,* is always used with the definite article when it refers to God the Father. When Greek wishes to express divinity it can use an adjective, *theion,* or it can choose to hold a middle position and use the noun, *theos,* but without the article. This verse really says: In the beginning was the Word and the Word was with the God and the Word was God (no article). In this way the author speaks of the Word as close to God as possible but does not completely identify the two. As we have already seen in our study, Jesus is equal to God and also dependent upon God.

Verse 2 may well be a repetition or even an addition and adds little to what precedes or follows.

Verse 3 shows us the role of the Word in creation. The Word was active in creation and actually entered into the activity. The Word creates as God's Son and creates all things so that nothing is seen as evil. All is good because all is created by God. Perhaps we have here a subtle apology against anyone who would denigrate the material in favor of the spiritual.

Verse 4 relates the Word to people. The Word is the mediator of God's most precious gifts: life and light. What makes a person a person is the gift of life, that which a person shares with all living things, and what distinguishes people from animals is intelligence or rationality or light.

Verse 5 shows a change in time in the poetic measure and may not pertain to the actual hymn. However, it bears a frequent theme of the gospel: the conflict between light and darkness, between good and evil and it carries the conviction that the darkness will never defeat the light. In other sections of the gospel we have seen how Nicodemus comes from the darkness to see Jesus (3.2) and Judas returns to the darkness when he decides to go through with the betrayal (13. 30).

Verses 6, 7, and 8 are clear additions and can be understood as a clever apologetic against those who still thought of John the Baptizer as the messiah.

Verse 9 is the continuation of verse 4 completing the idea of giving enlightenment as well as giving life.

Verses 10 and 11 are poignant: the world did not recognize the Word and even his very own (a favorite with John) do not recognize the Word. People had been prepared for the coming of God's Word in human form since the Word had been expressed in creation but in spite of this preparation those whom you would have expected to recognize the Word – his very own people– did not.

Verse 12 is the happy refrain: many did accept him but unfortunately some did not. The emphasis on this verse is not on any ethical activity but rather on people recognizing what they truly are, God's children. They are only to believe in the name of the Lord and that in itself will bring them to a realization of what is their destiny, to be God's family.

Verse 13 continues the thought of verse 12. God the Father is the one who will bring people to faith. No human power alone can accomplish this great gift. To be born of the power of God brings salvation and that alone. Textually this verse offers an interesting problem. Some of the later Latin manuscripts and some other earlier witnesses as well, have a singular verb in this verse rather than a plural. If a singular verb is original then the verb refers not to those coming to faith but to the Word himself who is born. This singular verb would then be seen as having reference to the birth of the Word made flesh, not from blood, nor the will of the flesh nor of the will of man, but by God. Could this possibly be a reference to the virginal conception of Jesus? For those who hold that the singular verb is original, that is the only response. The problem, however, remains. None of the early Greek manuscripts have a singular verb; they all have a plural and it is easier for us to understand why a scribe would change a plural verb to a singular (to bring this gospel in accord with the witness of Luke and Matthew with the virginal conception) than to understand why a scribe would change a singular to a plural. I mention this textual problem since it is a good illustration of what good scriptural scholarship must accomplish.

Verse 14 is the culmination of the hymn. The Word pitched his tent among us. The imagery is reminiscent of the Old Testament tradition in which God is present in the tabernacle that is portable and can be carried wherever the people travel. The Word will be with his people no matter where they travel. The notion of tent also connotes a temporary presence. The Word will be with us as incarnate only for a time. He must return to where he belongs and indeed from whence he has never left. When he has returned we will experience his Spirit with us who will take up a permanent indwelling with those who have become children of God through faith.

The use of "flesh" is also significant. The prologue contains the major themes of the gospel and it would be surprising if the author did not place some reference to the glorification of Jesus on the cross. The Greek word for flesh, *sarx,* can carry a sacrificial overtone. On the cross the Word made flesh offers himself for the sake of others so that they may become more faithful.

The reference to glory in this verse also strikes a familiar theme of the gospel. The glory of God in the Old Testament is always the manifestation of his goodness and power. This manifestation, moreover, is associated with the covenantal virtues of mercy and fidelity, which also can be translated as grace and truth. In the Word become flesh we have seen the power and goodness of God. We have seen the compassion of God, his kindness, his forgiveness and his fidelity even when we were not worthy of that fidelity.

Verse 15 is another addition continuing the reference to John the Baptizer.

Verse 16 completes the thought of verse 14. There is a superabundance of God's graciousness for all, that which the Word has received and that which the Word imparts.

Verse 17 should be seen as another addition, an editorial comment on verse 16.

The final verse has the Word back with the Father. The Word has completed his mission of revealing God the Father to all who will respond. The Word has become flesh and has also become the Son to the one Father of all.

The theology of the prologue includes the basic thought of John: Jesus, the Word become flesh is the revelation of the Father. He has come into a dark and evil world and has offered to people the possibility of moving from darkness to light. Those who accept the offer become part of God's family. Jesus accomplished his revelation by manifesting God's glory through his mercy and fidelity. We have seen him for a while and have come to believe in him as God's Son. The Word is a divine being even while the Word has also taken on the flesh common to all of us.

As the gospel unfolds the reader will come to appreciate these basic themes at greater depth. The evangelist will return repeatedly to the same offer of faith, each time deepening its meaning and drawing more people into its realm of influence. The great overture of the gospel is ended to be repeated in faint and in strong tones throughout the gospel.

SUGGESTIONS FOR REFLECTION

1. Jesus as the Word is with God but differs from God. How does this affect your understanding of Jesus? Your prayer life?

2. Can Jesus be equal to the Father and still not equal? Is this not a contradiction?

3. What role did the "Word" play in creation? Is the Word the example after which all was created?

4. Light and life are necessary for human life. Where do light and life originate according to the prologue? How does Jesus give life and light?

5. The witness to the Baptist in the prologue places the Baptist on a different plane when compared to Jesus. What role does the Baptist play here and in the rest of the gospel?

6. "The Word became flesh and made his dwelling among us" describes many aspects of Johannine theology. Why are these ideas important for understanding the Johannine Jesus?

7. Grace and truth are Old Testament concepts. In examining them, how would you relate them to the meaning of Christianity?

8. Jesus as the Word never leaves the Father. What implications are found in this statement?

9. The prologue offers themes that will recur in the gospel. What basic gospel themes can you find in this prologue?

10. Why is this prologue a good introduction to the gospel?

CHAPTER VI

THE SACRAMENTS
IN THE FOURTH GOSPEL

The presence or absence of references to sacraments in the Fourth Gospel has occupied scholars for years. Some find references to the sacraments throughout the gospel while others deny their very presence. If the gospel emphasized so strongly the need for personal faith, then what role might sacraments play? Are there clear references to baptism and the eucharist and if so, how are these sacraments presented in this gospel?

BAPTISM IN THE FOURTH GOSPEL

The author of this gospel knew Christian baptism. He did allude to the baptism of Jesus even if he chose not to narrate the event. The dialogue with Nicodemus seems to have some reference to baptism and other references to water (the blind man in chapter 9, the foot washing in chapter 13, and the water from the side of Christ in chapter 19) might carry some baptismal overtones. Each instance merits some study.

JOHN'S BAPTISM

Please read: John 3.22-36

The allusion to the baptism of Jesus in chapter 1 and the final witness of John to Jesus (3.22-26) seems to manifest the author's interest in the new baptism of the Spirit over against the water-baptism of John. He implies that John actually baptized Jesus, especially when we compare this account with that of the Synoptics. Still, he does not mention an actual baptism by water. The following verse clarifies the position of the author when he has John the Baptizer distinguishing his baptism from the messianic baptism of the Spirit. In verse 32 the Spirit descends and remains on Jesus, a distinctive characteristic of the messiah. We cannot draw definite conclusions from this text other than the general notion that in the context in which the author could have mentioned the actual baptism of Jesus, he chose to emphasize the coming of the Spirit on Jesus and the remaining of the Spirit on Jesus. The context implies baptism but the text ignores the actual ritual of baptism.

NICODEMUS AND BAPTISM

Please read: John 3.1-15

The dialogue with Nicodemus also seems to have reference to baptism. The burden of Jesus' remarks, however, concern the entering into the kingdom of God by being born from above (or again) and being begotten of Spirit. The author tells us why we must be born from above: the flesh can beget flesh while spirit begets spirit. If an individual desires to move from the natural level of life to the divine level, then God must raise him. Just as in the creation of humankind, God breathed his Spirit into the lifeless form to give life, so in this new creation the new gift of life must be communicated through the divine Spirit. Jesus can communicate this life-giving Spirit because he is the heavenly Son of Man who has descended from heaven (3. 13).

The primary meaning of the text does not refer to baptism of water but to the eschatological begetting through the outpouring of the Spirit of God made possible through Jesus. Nicodemus could have understood the reference to the outpouring of the Spirit since it frequently occurs in the Old Testament (Is 4.4; Zc 12.10; 13.11; Ez 36.25-27). A reference to baptism by water could hardly be understood in the dialogue and probably can be accounted for by a later understanding.

One verse does seem to imply water baptism: "No one can enter into God's kingdom without being begotten of water and Spirit" (3.5). This should be contrasted with John 3.3: "No one can see the reign of God unless he is begotten from above"; and also with John 3.8: "So it is with everyone begotten of the Spirit." The presence of "water and" in verse 5 when compared to the general meaning of the dialogue has encouraged some exegetes to conclude that these words are an addition. The problem with that opinion is the lack of early manuscript evidence to support it.

Some argue for a baptismal tone by claiming that faith in the Son of Man is concretized in the act of baptism. Others recognize the tenuous status of the words "water and" and argue that this verse existed in the tradition of the evangelist without a reference to water. The evangelist added "water and" to make the text speak of baptism. The gospel can then lay claim to faith as necessary for baptism and vice versa.

The likelihood that verse 5 refers to water baptism seems acceptable: the text does stipulate baptism as a means of rebirth through faith. The question of whether the words "water and" were added remains debatable. Since no early manuscript evidence supports this opinion and since often those who favor such an opinion do so for ideological reasons the following position seems attractive: somewhere in the process of Johannine tradition the rebirth by the Spirit, the basic meaning of the text, became associated with the act of water baptism. The text does contain a reference to water baptism but belongs to a tradition that emerged later in the Johannine community. The earliest tradition emphasized the role of the Spirit and faith. Since this is primary, water baptism alone never suffices.

FEAST OF TABERNACLES / WATER FROM THE SIDE

Please read: John 7.37-39; 19.34

On the feast of tabernacles Jesus stood up and cried: "If anyone thirsts, let him come to me; let him drink who believes in me. Scripture has it: 'From within him rivers of living water shall flow.' "

Some Bibles may have a slight variation from this text because of a difference in punctuation. The verse can also read: "Let him come and let him drink. He who believes in him, as scripture has it, from within him shall flow rivers of living water." From whom does the living water flow: from Jesus or from the believer, or does John wish to imply from both?

The verse continues with reference to the Spirit. The author informs us that Jesus was speaking of the Spirit which was yet to be given since Jesus had not yet been glorified. When we compare this verse with the flow of water from the side of Jesus in chapter 19.34, we might conclude that the handing over of his Spirit to the Beloved Disciple and his mother in chapter 19.30, together with the reference to water from his side, is the fulfillment of the prediction in chapter 7. Water in chapter 7 refers to the Spirit. This interpretation need not seem odd since often in the Old Testament water designated the Spirit. Obviously, however, we cannot quickly identify the water in chapter 7 with baptismal water. We do know that the early Fathers of the Church did indeed see in this text a reference to baptism.

In the seventh chapter the evangelist interrupted his narrative to remark that by water, Jesus meant the Spirit which his followers would receive after he had been glorified. The flow of water from his side, thus from within him, fulfills this prophecy since it takes place when he is glorified. Verse 19.35 with reference to belief relates this flow of water from Jesus' side to that of the seventh chapter and the call to faith.

BLOOD FROM THE SIDE

Please read: 1 John 5.6-8

The reference to blood from Jesus' side causes more problems. We can study the remarks in the First Epistle of John and see that the common elements are water, blood, spirit, and testimony. We know that baptism by John did not give the Spirit. The real begetting from water and the Spirit would be accomplished when Jesus was glorified (Jn 7.39). But the Spirit could not be given until Jesus had departed (Jn 16.7), until he had died or had shed his blood. In the phrasing of the epistle, the water had to be mingled with the blood before the Spirit could give testimony. Thus in the gospel picture of the flow of blood and water from the side of Christ, John informs us that now the Spirit can be given because Jesus has died and through his death he has gained the glory that was his before the world began (Jn 17.5). The lance demonstrated the truth of his death and made the affirmation of death the paradoxical beginning of life. From the dead Jesus comes forth living water, the Spirit, to all who will believe in him.

We can conclude from studying these passages that the author of the gospel relates the pouring forth of the water from the side of Christ in prophecy (Jn 7.37-39) and in actuality (Jn 19.34) to the gift of the Spirit which Jesus gave when he was glorified. Since, however, the gift of the Spirit was associated with baptism in the Johannine community (Jn 3.3) the author refers to baptism at least obliquely. Also the mention of water alone would bring to mind such an association for the early Church. What remains foremost, however, is the meaning of the life-giving Spirit accepted in faith.

THE BLIND MAN

Please read: John 9.1-8

We have already studied the blind man as a representative figure. The reference to water may not at first sight seem very sacramental in tone. Clearly the early Church interpreted this chapter as baptismal, but does the text give us any hints as to the accuracy of that interpretation?

John narrates the miracle in two verses. He describes the gestures of Jesus but the man sees only when he washed in the pool. Since the man's physical blindness contrasts with the sin of spiritual blindness (Jn 9.39) and the evangelist emphasized the fact that the man had been *born* blind (Jn 9.1, 2, 13, 18, 19, 20, 24) the evangelist seems to be playing on the idea that the man was born in sin (Jn 9.2, 34). Even if Jesus denies such a charge (Jn 9.3) this sin of blindness can be removed only by bathing in the water of the pool of Siloam.

The author also pauses to tell us the meaning of the name of the pool: "one who has been sent." Since in this gospel Jesus is the one who has been sent by the Father (Jn 3. 17, 34; 5. 36, etc.) the pool is associated with Jesus. Water from this pool was used during the Jewish feast of tabernacles, a harvest feast, and on that occasion Jesus had remarked that he was the source of life-giving water.

The man in sin must be washed in the pool. Here and only here does the evangelist afford power to the water but not in a magical sense since the use of the interpretation of the word Siloam binds the water to Jesus himself. The implicit reference to the feast of tabernacles further emphasizes the role of Jesus in accomplishing the healing of the man. He needed to be washed to be healed. Jesus caused the healing but used water. The baptismal overtones are strong but once again, the place of faith seems primary.

THE FOOT WASHING

Please read: John 13. 1-20

The foot washing can be understood as sacramental or not. The impetus to seek some sacramental meaning comes not from the choice of words themselves, nor the context but rather from the importance given to the foot washing by Jesus: without it we can have no share in his heritage (13. 8). The act of humiliation does not suffice to secure the loss of heritage. This fact has encouraged scholars to find some sacramental implication in the event, but is that the only possible explanation?

Since Jesus said he must wash Peter, we are not involved with simply an example to be imitated but a salvific action of Jesus. If the foot washing can be a symbol of the salvific death of the Lord, then the importance of participating in the action becomes intelligible. The presence of humility need not be completely deleted since this is the interpretation given by the evangelist himself (13. 14, 15) but the symbol is prophetic of the humiliating death of the Son of God for the forgiveness of sins. The opening statement of passing to the Father and and concluding with the foot washing with the reference to the betrayal of Jesus, situates the incident in the context of the death of Jesus.

Jesus provoked Peter to question him which gave Jesus the opportunity to explain the salvific necessity of his death; it would bring people a share in his heritage and would cleanse them from sin. This explanation, however, does not settle the question of some sacramental implication.

The mere mention of washing does not connote baptism. If the major meaning is soteriological, we need not seek other allusions unless the text itself clearly suggests a further quest. The only possibility of arguing to the presence of some baptismal overtones comes not from the foot washing itself, but the meaning of the footwashing as prophesying the death of Jesus. If the death of Jesus enables him to give his Spirit (Jn 19. 34) then the reference to the death of Jesus in this passage in symbolic form with the added claim that this accomplishes a share in his heritage, could possibly be related to baptism through association with John 7. 37-39 and 3. 5. Perhaps the stronger sacramental meaning is the eucharist. If the foot washing refers to the death of the Lord and the eucharist has a similar salvific effect, then the foot washing can also refer to the eucharist.

THE EUCHARIST IN THE FOURTH GOSPEL

Please read: John 6. 1-59

The eucharistic interpretation of chapter 6 creates one of the most debated issues in Johannine sacramentality. Some find a primary eucharistic meaning throughout the chapter; others admit the presence of a eucharistic tone but in a secondary mode; still others limit the eucharist to verses 51-58 and claim that these verses are from the hand of a final editor. Additional problems face the reader: did Jesus speak these words on the historical occasion of the multiplication of the loaves, or did the evangelist construct the speech? Does the entire discourse refer to the teaching of Jesus as the Word of God with a fundamental Wisdom motif? Can we find a clear distinction between Wisdom and eucharist in the discourse or not?

Some eucharistic overtones appear in the miracle of the multiplication of the loaves. A comparison with the Synoptic accounts and that of John demonstrates that the wording of the multiplication was colored by eucharistic liturgies familiar to the various communities. "To give thanks" appears in the miracle and at the Last Supper in the Synoptics. Jesus himself distributes the loaves as he does the bread at the Last Supper. The use of "gather up" and the reference to the "fragments" find parallels in the eucharistic prayer of the *Didache,* an early Church document.

In the first section of the discourse the bread which has come down from heaven is Jesus as the Word of God. Jesus offers his word as bread and he must be accepted in faith. John situates the teaching of Jesus in the context of messianic hopes. We have another Exodus experience with Jesus offering the interpretation. The true bread is not the manna in the desert but what gives life to the world (Jn 6. 33). Jesus, like Wisdom of old, invites all to come and recline (Prv 9. 5; Eccl 24. 20; Is 55. 1-3). Jesus alone gives life to those who believe in him; an immortal life.

Jesus expects a reaction of faith (Jn 6. 35, 36, 40, 47) or a coming to him which also means faith. Jesus cites Isaiah 54. 13: "They shall all be taught by God" (Jn 6.45) which brings out the sapiential symbolism of the bread. We might also recall that the nearest parallel for the bread of life is the living water in chapters 4 and 7 and water symbolizes the revelation that calls for faith.

We should note in particular verses 36-40. They spell out the need to believe in Jesus and to accept the will of the Father that all should have life through him. We also have the present eschatology here: everyone who believes in the Son has eternal life even while he awaits the raising up on the last day (we shall return to this eschatology later). We have seen these themes before: the Father works to bring individuals to Jesus but the individual must personally accept Jesus in faith. The result of the faith is the gift of eternal life now and in the future.

The final section of the bread of life discourse informs us that eternal life comes not only from believing but from feeding on his flesh and drinking his blood (Jn 6. 54). The role of the Father recedes. Now Jesus is the principal agent for life. The vocabulary also has changed: eat, flesh, drink, blood. The stress on eating the flesh and drinking the blood cannot be a metaphor for accepting the revelation of Jesus but must refer to the eucharist. These words of Jesus have the same meaning as the ones recorded in the institution account of Matthew: "Take this and eat it; this is my body . . . drink . . . this is my blood" (Mt 26.26-28).

A second indication to support the eucharistic interpretation is the formula in verse 51: "the bread I will give is my flesh, for the life of the world". This resembles the Lukan formula for institution: "This is my body to be given for you" (Lk 22. 19). Even the announcement of the treason of Judas which follows (Jn 6. 71) adds another link to the Last Supper of the Synoptics.

Clearly these verses are manifestations of eucharistic teaching in the Gospel of John whether they are historically related to the multiplication of the loaves or not. If, however, we separate the discourse on the eucharist from the earlier discourse which seems to imply a Wisdom motif, what might have prompted the author to join and juxtapose the two discourses: the one on the bread of life as Wisdom demanding faith, and the other on the eucharist which we would have expected to have found in the farewell discourses at the Last Supper?

Some scholars suggest that the second discourse with its clear eucharistic theme serves to bring out the eucharistic meaning which is latent and secondary in the first discourse. But might not the opposite be true: the first gives the meaning and the interpretation of the second. The eucharistic teaching in this chapter continues the tendency of Wisdom literature to call people to faith and involves the religious aspirations of all.

The author of the gospel presents the meaning of the eucharist as the general meaning of the coming of Jesus. Thus, the meaning of the Christian life may be summed up and expressed in the eucharist, but the eucharist can never be separated from its context: the presence in human history of Jesus as the revealer and mediator of life is primary. To him people must respond in faith made possible through the action of the Father who calls people to his Son. With this presupposition the eucharist can have meaning and can be the bread of life which gives eternal life to those who have believed. The eucharist in the Fourth Gospel interprets the coming of Jesus himself, and vice versa. All must be accepted as the work of the Father in giving his Son for the life of the world. The eucharist makes sense for the author of John if we accept it as the memorial of the redeeming Incarnation. Even the eucharist takes its meaning from the fundamental christology of the Fourth Gospel.

CONCLUSION

The strongest reference to baptism as a ritual we have discovered in chapter 9. The discourse with Nicodemus referred originally to baptism in the Spirit and not water baptism. However, early in the Johannine tradition the baptism of water was related, at least in the consciousness of the author, to the baptism in the Spirit. The references to water in chapters 7 and 19 refer principally to the gift of the Spirit.

The only passage clearly referring to the eucharist is found in chapter 6. The eucharistic overtones of the miracle of the loaves common to all the evangelists sets the scene for a full eucharistic teaching in verses 51-58 but this is further interpreted by the bread of life discourse which concentrates on faith in Jesus.

The Fourth Gospel presents some signs of sacramental activity and teaching which might be judged explicit in their own right but must be judged as implicit when compared to the Synoptics. Matthew (26.26-29), Mark (14.22-25), and Luke (22. 17-20) include the institution of the eucharist at the Last Supper. Matthew also has the instruction to baptize all nations (Mt 28. 19). The longer ending of Mark refers to baptism for salvation (Mk 16. 16). What might have prompted the author of John to place the sacramental activity of his community in such an oblique position? If the presence of some teaching on baptism and the eucharist seems evident, why is the ritual omitted?

The author of this gospel has his own peculiar interpretation of the sacraments to emphasize their spiritual value and to relate the sacraments to faith. We have already noted some internal conflicts within the early Church communities. The original sign source of the gospel was judged incomplete since belief in Jesus as a miracle worker never suffices. We must believe in him as God's Son. At this period of Church development we have evidence for a developing hierarchical Church. These factors coupled with the basic thrust of the gospel—the individual response of faith in Jesus as the revealer of God—will help explain the apparent lack of interest by the author of the gospel in explicit sacramental references.

The presence of baptism and the eucharist in the Church take their meaning from the faith of the community in Jesus. Just as belief in him as a miracle worker never sufficed, so a water baptism will not suffice unless it takes its meaning from belief in Jesus as manifested by the presence of his Spirit. If people go to the font to be healed of their blindness, the font is Jesus himself and the healing is the result of faith.

The meaning of the eucharist depends upon a previous acceptance of Jesus as Wisdom. Only then can we "eat his flesh and drink his blood."

If the early Church had already fallen into the temptation of emphasizing ritual over meaning, which is the danger of any organized Church, the Gospel of John reminded those communities as well as the contemporary communities, to be careful not to lose the fundamental: personal faith in the Lord.

SUGGESTIONS FOR REFLECTION

1. The position of eucharistic teaching in chapter 6 is unusual. Does the explanation help in understanding the eucharist?

2. Some see the foot washing as eucharistic. How can the foot washing relate to the eucharist?

3. Is wisdom necessary for the celebration of the eucharist?

4. Worship in spirit and truth is the touchstone of worship in this gospel. How does this apply today?

5. Do the eucharistic overtones in the multiplication of the loaves give us any insights into eucharistic overtones in any celebration of an ordinary meal?

6. Does the eucharistic teaching in chapter 6 mean that none can be saved unless they celebrate the eucharist?

7. The theme of rebirth in the Spirit in chapter 3 is a broader concept than that of the sacrament of baptism. How does this affect your understanding of the sacrament? Is rebirth the same as baptism in the Spirit as understood in the charismatic movement?

8. Do you see any references to baptism in chapter 9? Why would the author relate the water to Jesus?

9. The other references to water in the gospel—are they clearly baptismal? What are some other possibilities?

10. Is this gospel sacramental in a broad context rather than sacramental with reference to the official sacraments of the Church?

11. How do the sacramental concepts in this gospel relate to the Church's present teachings about the sacraments?

CHAPTER VII

THE ESCHATOLOGY
OF THE FOURTH GOSPEL

Usually the word "eschatology" connotes the last things: death, judgment, heaven, hell. The word comes from the Greek word *eschaton,* meaning last or final.

To talk about the eschatology of the Fourth Gospel and see the meaning in relation to the last things can cause some confusion since the gospel seems to take the future and bring it into the present. In one sense, there are no last things for they have already been realized.

Throughout the gospel Jesus brings salvation and in this offer of salvation an individual must decide to accept or fall into judgment. The salvation and judgment is promised to the individual here and now. The whole of Johannine theology is marked with this tendency: with Jesus the hour of salvation has arrived, finally and irrevocably (Jn 4.23; 5.25). The eschatology is already realized, it belongs to the present since the outlook is dominated by the presence of Christ. John shifts the focus from the future to the present and even when the Johannine Jesus is apparently talking about the future, in reality the life of the community in the present with the presence of the Paraclete is the real focus.

FUTURE ESCHATOLOGY
Please read: John 5.28-29; 6.39, 40, 44, 57; 12.48

A careful reading of the gospel, however, shows that some passages do refer to the future resurrection and judgment.

73

The revelatory discourse in chapter 5 contains a reference to the raising of the dead (5. 28-29); chapter 6 has four stereotyped sayings: "I will raise him up on the last day"(6. 39, 40, 44, 57) and the same is found in John 12.48 though here it refers to judgment.

For some these references to the future are clear additions coming from an editor who wished to make this unusual gospel acceptable to the then developing, more orthodox Church. The real importance of these passages is whether the reference to future eschatology is in general conflict with the thinking of the evangelist. To try to assess this demands an understanding of the more general approach to eschatology in the gospel: why does the evangelist emphasize the present?

ETERNAL LIFE

> *Please read: John 3.15; 4.36; 5.39; 6.54-58;*
> *10.28; 12.25; 17.1-4*

Salvation in the Fourth Gospel is eternal life which the believer already has. The believer will pass through this world, the realm of darkness and death, to enter into the heavenly realm to share in the salvation of God.

In the gospel God is the one who has life and he gives it to the Son who in turn offers it to others, but we can also see the reversal of this process. People search for salvation, for life, and they find it through belief in Jesus. We even have a definition of eternal life: "Eternal life is this: to know you, the only true God, and him whom you have sent, Jesus Christ" (17.3). The mission God entrusted to Jesus his Son means eternal life for people. As eternal life or salvation is the goal of human existence, it will be accomplished in the knowledge of God and Jesus Christ. Knowledge here should not be construed in some rational or theoretical sense; it means an inner apprehension and participation and, ultimately in the Gospel of John, a communion.

74

Left alone no one can break out of the darkness that limits thinking and acting (3.31). Faith in the one who can open the eye to divine life fulfills a longing that all experience. The promise of this life is not postponed to some distant future, but it is a life here and now on earth; in this human life the believer can see the transcendence of his being and can be sure of his enduring security in the God who is the source of life. The believer also is expected to put this life into action by living, as we have already seen, a life of love of the brethren.

JUDGMENT IN THE PRESENT

Please read: John 3.18-21; 5.22-30; 8.16-26

The contrasting concept of judgment is also brought into the present. Though judgment still appears as divine judgment, (8.50; 12.31) and it is given to the Son to judge as God had previously judged (5.22, 27), human responsibility is more heavily emphasized. People must come to a decision to move from the darkness of sin and death to the light of faith and life. If people choose to remain in the darkness they have brought judgment upon themselves; if others choose to move to the light they have already been judged; they have passed from darkness to light. The judgment that is referred to God is only the ratification of what has already taken place on the human level. People have brought this judgment upon themselves (3.18-21). When one decides against faith, then God has no other possibility than to ratify a personal choice. The word of Jesus which is meant to be a word of salvation becomes a word of judgment and condemnation. When a person freely withdraws from God and chooses to remain in sin and death (5.24) the person passes a death judgment upon himself or herself. No future judgment can be envisioned for that has already taken place in human life. When a person ultimately dies, there is no final judgment but only a fulfillment of a judgment brought on by personal decision in life.

RESURRECTION ON THE LAST DAY

Please read: John 11.23-26

If anyone thinks that the theology of John still allows for a future eschatology to be fulfilled in a perfect way in the future, on the last day, the study of John 11.23-26 removes any doubt. Martha introduces the Jewish expectation of the resurrection at the last day. Jesus gives another interpretation. Jesus himself is the resurrection and the life; here and now in the presence of Jesus resurrection is actually taking place. In this very hour the dead are hearing the voice of the Son of God and those who hear him in faith come to life and no longer die for all eternity. The culmination of this teaching is Lazarus himself who comes forth from the tomb on hearing the word of Jesus.

MEANING OF JOHANNINE ESCHATOLOGY

Discussions on the meaning of the present and future eschatology of the Gospel of John began some time ago and continue today. Some dismiss all the references to the future as secondary additions; others see the need for a final completion of eschatology, begun in this life, but brought to perfection in another. Perhaps it is better not to try to take sides but rather to admit that the general outlook of the Fourth Gospel is to the present even if there are some references to a future, whether from the hand of the evangelist or from an editor.

The previous study of the passages involved do not dismiss the idea of a future but stress in relation to the sending of Jesus the idea that he is come to save now and not to judge. Judgment itself does remain and perhaps paradoxically we can say that Jesus does judge (5.30; 8.16), but only after an individual has chosen unbelief. A decision in the present in favor of belief or unbelief is itself the initial judgment. The author does not wish to enter into a polemic against judgment in the future as much as to emphasize the importance of salvation now because of the presence of Jesus in human history.

The same holds true for resurrection. In Jesus the Jewish hope for fulfillment in resurrection has already taken place. The Christian belief in resurrection far surpasses all previous Jewish expectations. Martha (11.27) is led from her merely future-oriented hope to faith in the bringer of salvation and giver of life in the present—a model for all who turn from the incompleteness of the old religion to Christian faith which alone brings the true fulfillment.

We cannot prove that the evangelist has deliberately rejected the primitive future eschatology of the Church, but we can come to appreciate why he concentrated on the present. For John, as for Paul, the crucial factor is personal faith in Jesus. Like Paul, John can also describe the Christian existence as life in faith but without the eschatological tension between the already and the not yet that is characteristic of Paul. But are we dealing only with a shift in emphasis or does the evangelist want to present a different theology?

The study of the individuals in this gospel has shown that the author is very much concerned with the fate of the individual believer. The individual confronts the meaning of his existence and the possibility of salvation through faith. Where salvation is concerned the individual stands out more prominently than in any other writing of the New Testament. This gives Johannine theology a certain existential flavor. In this approach the interest would inevitably shift from the future of the world or of the human race or even the Church as the community of faith, to the individual and his or her fate. The idea of entering through faith into the world of Jesus is more important and even takes over the function of the parousia as the completion of all. This change in perspective or perhaps personal attitude can help us to understand the Johannine lack of interest in the future and the final things. For John the coming of Jesus is itself the eschatological event. The christology is not a function of the eschatology but the eschatology is a function of the christology. The fullness of salvation exists in Jesus (1.14, 16); he offers this to humankind definitively and permanently (17.3) made accessible to all in faith (20. 31). The decision made now brings about salvation and judgment and includes in itself the totality of the future. Perhaps even the disciples of the Beloved Disciple could not long maintain such a firm conviction about the reality of salvation and began to look to the future to confirm what had already happened, and so they spoke of the resurrection to life and the judgment on the evildoers (5. 28-29).

What the eschatology of the Fourth Gospel can teach the Church today is the need to contemplate the meaning of life and the search for personal existence. The future can be less important if we all focus on the present reality, the fulfilled promise of salvation through faith. Wherever the history of humankind is leading, or however an "end" may come, humankind can never again fall out of the love of God who sent his only Son so that they might live with his life for all eternity.

78

SUGGESTIONS FOR REFLECTION

1. Does Jesus give life through his word? Is this eternal life?

2. If judgment is already present how would such a teaching affect the understanding of the sacrament of penance?

3. Does a realized eschatology respond to people's needs? Why might it be important for the Church today?

4. Can we lose a sense of a future with a realized eschatology? How can both aspects of eschatology be harmonized? Why would the Gospel of John have wanted to have both types as present?

5. Does concern about death, judgment, heaven, and hell give any insight into people's attitudes toward these experiences?

6. Why would people benefit from coming and living in the light?

7. Does a realized eschatology affect your understanding of how you should live?

8. If eternal life is now, is there an afterlife?

9. Should Christians live their lives based upon the Gospel of John even if there were no afterlife?

10. What makes you more comfortable: a realized eschatology or a future eschatology?

CHAPTER VIII

THE PASSION OF JESUS

The title for this chapter might seem misleading. When we think of the passion of the Lord we usually think of the painful experience that Jesus endured from the agony in the garden through the actual crucifixion and death. The Synoptics display, at times in a graphic way, the suffering of the Lord as he faced his death. I say the title for this chapter is misleading since in the Gospel of John, Jesus does not suffer. The road to Calvary is a glorious parade leading to the final hour of glory when he dies having fulfilled all that was expected of him and communicates his spirit on the Beloved Disciple and upon his mother.

Please read: John 18

The chapter begins with Jesus in the garden but unlike the Synoptics there is no prayer to the Father asking to be released from this hour. Jesus does not suffer but is in complete control of the situation. His captors, along with the betrayer, enter the garden to apprehend him but it is clear that Jesus is in complete command of the situation. The confrontation is between Jesus and the powers of darkness. Judas and the soldiers come out of the night and meet the powerful Lord Jesus who answers their question and immediately they fall to the ground.

When Jesus meets Pilate the nature of his own Kingship becomes evident: Jesus is king by bearing witness to the truth, this same truth which makes all free (8.32). God is present in

Jesus freeing people from the power of darkness and inviting them to come to the light and be free. Pilate appears in this chapter as basically a good, if weak, man and asks Jesus: "What is truth?" (18.38). Secular power is indifferent to the truth and freedom that Jesus offers. Faith alone is the response to the truth that Jesus offers and Pilate is unable to offer that response.

CRUCIFIXION

Please read: John 19. 1-42

Unlike the Jesus of the Synoptics who needs assistance in bearing his cross, Jesus in this gospel bears the cross alone. The parade has begun that will lead to the glorification in his death, and the chief participant will control his own destiny and fulfill what is expected of him.

At the base of the cross are the two most faithful followers: his mother and the Beloved Disciple. They hear his final testimony and accept the Spirit that he will communicate to them.

Aware that he had accomplished all that was expected of him he announced it is finished and bowing his head he handed over his Spirit to those who were present to receive it.

THE PASSION IN JOHN AND THE SYNOPTICS

In the passion account the Gospel of John comes closest to the accounts of the ministry of Jesus as found in the Synoptics. The passion, death, and resurrection of Jesus are the aspects of the meaning of Jesus that were quickly established in the Church's tradition. But even here there are distinctive features.

To understand the peculiar approach of John we should note the following events which we associate with the passion which are found only in the Synoptics and not in the Gospel of John:

82

agony in the garden
kiss of Judas
flight of the disciples
process before the Sanhedrin
derision of Jesus as a prophet
Simon of Cyrene
derision of Jesus on the cross
darkness
cry of the dying Jesus
rending of the temple veil
faith of the centurion

Many of these can quickly be eliminated from the Johannine theology precisely because of his emphasis on the divinity of Jesus, the all-knowing savior who determines his own destiny.

The following events found only in John can also be understood against the background of the Johannine christology:

powerful word of Jesus in the garden: "I am"
interrogation before Annas
first altercation between Pilate and the Jews
private interrogation by Pilate
refusal to change the title on the cross
presence of his mother and the Beloved Disciple
"I thirst"
"it is finished"
piercing of the side
ministration of Nicodemus

The Synoptics view the death of Jesus as the end, a painful, sorrowful end. John sees the crucifixion in light of the risen Lord. The passion and death are anticipations and signs of his glorification since on the cross you see the results of the work of salvation (12. 32; 13. 1) The passion of Jesus is a triumph. The atmosphere is that of glory and so the cross is the throne of the kingdom from which the powerful savior will reign and will communicate his spirit.

Please read: John 3. 28; 12. 32

The Synoptics have predictions of the passion of the Lord during his ministry with the idea that it was necessary for Jesus to suffer and die. John says it is necessary and fitting for Jesus not to die but to be exalted. The word crucify is found only in the narration of the facts.

The word exaltation is related to Isaiah 52. 13: the servant shall be exalted and raised up very high. The same idea is found in Acts 2.33 and 5.31, but for Luke it refers to the ascension after death. John used the word not in relationship to an ascension after death but to an exaltation in death.

John 3.14 refers first to the cross, which indicates the necessity of faith to recognize this strange death as an exaltation. The result is the gift of life to those who will respond in faith to the exaltation in death.

John 8. 28 connects exaltation with the Son of Man. The formula is both biblical and prophetic, expressing a twofold effect: the description of the action of God bringing either salvation or punishment. God manifests himself to his people and then must be recognized by them in faith. The cross is then the revelation that is offered to people to believe in Jesus or to refuse to believe. The raising up, the exaltation reveals Jesus to all who are receptive.

John 12. 32 finds its Old Testament counterpart in Jeremiah 31. 3ff. The context is the restoration of the messianic people. The theme of gathering together is important for John since the people who believe are united both in love and in faith.

Jesus as exalted on the cross, with the title of king over his head, manifests the regality of Jesus. It is he who overcomes the prince of this world and its darkness. God the Father has established in Jesus a force that will draw people, and in faith they will gather around the cross as the messianic congregation predicted and hoped for by the Old Testament prophets.

On the cross the fruits of salvation are made evident in the exercise of the regal power of Jesus. People of faith are persuaded and freely attracted to come to the cross, see its meaning, and experience the saving presence of God in Jesus, which will give them a value and purpose in life. The exaltation draws people of faith.

THE HOUR OF JESUS

Usually the "hour" is an eschatological theme designating the time of salvation, but even in the Synoptic gospel it refers to the passion of Jesus (Mk 14. 41).

Please read: John 4. 21-23; 5. 23; 16. 25

In these passages the meaning is broad and can be seen in the more general and eschatological sense. The Samaritan woman is reminded that the future eschatological hour has already come. This conveys something of the understanding of eschatology that we have already noted in this gospel. The same idea is present when Jesus refers to the dead hearing the voice of the Son of God, and the eschatological hour when Jesus will speak plainly of the Father. While these ideas have a broad meaning in the gospel, the more specific meaning refers to the passion, and in particular, the crucifixion of the Lord.

Please read: John 2. 4; 7. 30; 8. 20; 12. 23-27;
13. 1; 17.1

In each of these instances the reference is to the final hour which is the hour of glorification on the cross. At Cana the time for true wine is his passion and exaltation; his enemies could not arrest him since it was not the time for the passion (7. 30; 8. 20). In chapter 12 we have some reminiscences of the agony in the garden since Jesus is troubled. The hour has come for him to be glorified. Jesus will battle with the forces of darkness and will conquer, but the passion is always joined to the glorification that will accompany it.

The opening verse of the farewell discourse (13. 1) introduces the final testament of Jesus. There will be no distinction in this gospel between the passion, death, and resurrection. All are united as one hour of triumph, and in John 17.1 the hour introduces the solemn priestly prayer of Jesus. The prayer of the hour is one of glorification.

The hour of the passion is not just an hour of his life but the final and eschatological hour of salvation which Jesus fulfills as messiah. This hour cannot be easily divided into episodes as in the Synoptics, especially in Luke, but must be seen as the consummation of the meaning of the Incarnation. As the gospel unfolds so does the understanding of his hour. At Cana the hour is indeterminate, but in chapter 7 the reference is clearly to his death. In the twelfth chapter the additional theme of glory is attached to the hour, and in the final two references (13.1; 17.1) all notion of death is gone, with the theme of glorification the only one.

By speaking of the hour of Jesus, the evangelist continued his basic eschatological stance of anticipating future events. All is fulfilled and completed as Jesus reigns as king from the cross on Calvary.

MODE OF JESUS' ACTING IN HIS PASSION

The ordinary understanding of the passion is to consider it psychologically and physiologically: the burdensome way of the cross is preceded by the psychological agony in the garden as well as the brutal treatment in the crowning with thorns and the scourging at the pillar. All this is foreign to John. John examines the passion theologically and soteriologically.

From the outset, Jesus knows all that will befall him: "Jesus, aware of all that would happen to him. . . " (18. 4). Just as Jesus alone knew the Father, so he alone knew his hour (13. 1; 18. 4). All that he does is accomplished in full awareness of what should be done: "After that, Jesus realizing that everything was now finished, said to fulfill the scripture, 'I am thirsty' " (19. 28). The Jesus of the passion in this gospel is not a passive victim or a reluctant captive. With full awareness of all of the events and their meaning for himself and for others, he controlled what was happening to him and brought them to the fulfillment expected of him in full liberty.

In this gospel Jesus always is serene. With full dignity he commands the soldiers in the garden; with a similar attitude he responds to Annas and remains a king in the presence of Pilate. The way of the cross is not a defeat but a triumph. The cross becomes the throne from which the king will reign. No sorrow, no suffering will mar the power and dignity of the only Son of God.

Christian theology often viewed the cross as expiatory, a sacrifice for sins. John sees the crucifixion as the presence of salvation and the full revelation of the meaning of Jesus. The goodness of God overwhelms us, for God has loved us in our sins. The sign of this goodness finds expression in the gift of Jesus as God's Son, even unto death. Jesus dies, but his death is more than what seems apparent. In truth, Jesus reigns in his death, for then he can communicate his Spirit to those who will receive it, and what better examples of faith to receive the Spirit than his mother and the Beloved Disciple. The passion according to John ends in triumph just as it began.

SUGGESTIONS FOR REFLECTION

1. Why did Jesus die, and why did he have to die such a cruel death?

2. Do you prefer the passion according to John with its distinctive approach, or the Synoptic versions? What makes them so different, and what is their peculiar value?

3. The Gospel of John is read on Good Friday. How would this affect the understanding of that celebration?

4. Why is the crucifixion the hour of glorification? Is this reading too much theology into the death of Jesus?

5. Jesus knows all and is always in control. How does this affect your understanding of the humanity of Jesus?

6. Jesus is king in his passion. In what sense can he be a king in his ministry and in the present Church?

7. The people cried "Crucify him!" Does this mean that Christians ought to blame the Jews for the death of Jesus?

8. When the Jews claim they have no king but Caesar, they repudiate their heritage for God was their king. Why would the author have wanted to emphasize this rejection of their heritage?

9. Jesus reigns from the cross and gives his Spirit. What role do the Beloved Disciple and his mother play in this scene?

CHAPTER IX

THE RESURRECTION APPEARANCES

The meaning of the resurrection of Jesus involves more than just a return to life. Resuscitation is not resurrection. With the resurrection Jesus enters into his final and definitive mode of existence. Now Jesus is messiah in power, able to communicate his Spirit to others (Acts 2. 36). Now that Jesus has transcended space and time and has lived and died as the one faithful Son of the Most High, everything in this world, especially human beings, can be the means by which he can further communicate with his followers.

Please read: John 20. 1-31

John does not emphasize the resurrection. His interest centered on the glorification which was the crucifixion. Jesus reigned from the cross and was exalted, glorified and actually communicated his Spirit to those present in faith. The resurrection expresses this new creation which was accomplished in the crucifixion. Now he can call his disciples brothers for the first time for now that they had received his Spirit they too could call God their Father as Jesus did.

The essential note to the resurrection appearances is the presence of Jesus to his friends when they were in need. In each instance after the resurrection the followers of Jesus experienced some problem; his very presence was enough to resolve their dilemma.

The chapter begins with Peter and the Beloved Disciple running to the tomb. The Beloved Disciple arrives first but allows Peter to enter first. Peter notes the carefully placed linen but is not depicted as a believer in the risen Lord. The Beloved Disciple sees and believes (20.8).

Mary Magdalene's visit to the tomb comes from a tradition independent from the tradition of the previous visit to the tomb by the two disciples. The writer uses the literary device of having angels ask Mary some questions. Mary is disconsolate for she believes that someone has stolen the body of Jesus. The theme of failing to recognize Jesus is present in other episodes in this gospel (Jn 21.4-7) and also in Luke (24.13-31). But when Jesus calls her by name, she immediately responds in faith. Just as the Good Shepherd knows his sheep by name and they respond to this voice, so the believer in Mary responds to the sound of the Master's voice as he calls her name.

Once she has recognized him Jesus instructs her not to continue to cling to him but, as in the case of the Samaritan woman, Jesus directs her to become a missionary to others. Mary will announce to the brothers of the Lord that he is risen. Jesus will leave them, but now they will continue to fulfill his mission.

The first reaction of the disciples was confusion and doubt at the reports of the risen Lord. Only the Beloved Disciple saw and believed (Jn 20.8). Mysteriously, Jesus comes to the disciples in the upper room. They had failed him and must have wondered what he would say when he saw them. Jesus arrives in an unusual way and wishes them only peace. In the midst of human failure and sin, Jesus offers forgiveness and hope for a better future. Into this context John has placed the commission to the Church to forgive sins.

This power to forgive sins is given to the whole community since the author stipulates that the "disciples" are gathered and not just the Twelve. Forgiveness is not a juridical process in this gospel but a proclamation of peace which looks to the future and a new existence. Peace will come when a person accepts his or her failure and relies on the mercy and forgiveness of God mediated through his Church in Jesus. For the first time the Gospel of John, in the context of the failure of the disciples to remain faithful to the Lord, refers to a forgiveness of sins as belonging to the Church.

Thomas, not present at the above appearance, is present a week later in a much troubled state. He doubts and wants to have the resurrection of the Lord clinically verified to his own satisfaction. The Lord appears to the troubled disciple and immediately he becomes the believer.

The final chapter contains the appearance of Jesus to the disciples while fishing, and the rehabilitation of Peter in the presence of the Beloved Disciple. We have already referred to the roles of these characters previously and shall return to them in the next chapter.

The material in this chapter is Johannine but some of it appears in the Synoptic tradition (Lk 5. 1-11; Mt 14. 28-33). Now the disciples will become fishers of men as they had previously been fishermen.

Jesus was glorified on Calvary. Now he will be present to his Church at all times, especially when his faithful ones are in need. The risen Lord, having become the faithful Son of God in death as in life, has completed his sojourn on earth. Now that he has accomplished his mission, as risen Lord he can fulfill his promise to be with his followers through the presence of the new Paraclete, the Spirit of truth who will guide them to all truth (Jn 16.13).

SUGGESTIONS FOR REFLECTION

1. Is Jesus really present to his friends when they are in need? Has this been your experience?

2. If the resurrection is not emphasized, how is the theology of the risen Lord expressed in the Gospel of John?

3. Jesus calls Mary by name. Why is this important in this gospel? How is this related to the Good Shepherd?

4. Belief in the risen Lord characterizes chapter 20. What does it mean to believe in the risen Lord? How is this belief present in the lives of believers today?

5. Mary becomes a missionary. The same was true for the Samaritan woman. Does this affect the role of women in the Church today? Could women have figured prominently in the Johannine community?

6. Penance and the forgiveness of sins is placed in a particular context in this gospel. How does this affect your understanding of forgiveness? Does this power belong to the entire Church or only Church leaders?

7. Peace is God's gift through Jesus in the midst of human failure and sin. How can the Church mediate it?

8. Why would the author of this gospel have altered and expanded the material common to the Synoptic tradition in chapter 20?

CHAPTER X

THE ROLE OF THE BELOVED DISCIPLE

Previously we have studied the Beloved Disciple as he appeared at the Last Supper (Jn 13. 21-26), at the foot of the cross (Jn 19. 25-27), in the dramatic race to the tomb (Jn 20. 2-10), and we also identified him with the "other disciple" in John 18. 15-16.

Please read: John 21

In chapter 21 he appears in two scenes alongside Peter. We have already noted that this chapter is from a hand other than that of the evangelist, with a distinctive approach to Johannine theology and need. The study of Peter and the Beloved Disciple in this chapter will help us to understand the situation of the Johannine community as it emerged and developed near the end of the first century or at the beginning of the second century.

The study of the Beloved Disciple in the gospel concluded that he was the epitome of believer, disciple, beloved, and witness. He probably was not one of the Twelve, but a close associate of Jesus, perhaps from Jerusalem. If this analysis of the Beloved Disciple in the body of the gospel presents him as an ideal follower of Jesus, this does not mean that he was not an historical figure. Rather, an historical personage stands behind the Beloved Disciple even if he has been idealized. His presence in this final chapter suggests that he played a most significant role in the Johannine community and had died recently (Jn 21.23-24). This final chapter was written in the context of that death.

The Beloved Disciple was the intimate of Jesus (Jn 13.23-30) and the one who would authenticate the testimony of the gospel (Jn 21.24). As such he had authority in his own right, and need not have been subservient to any other type of early Church authority. When he is juxtaposed with Peter in the final chapter a question of the relationship between the two leaders arises.

PETER IN JOHN 21

Peter in this final chapter receives a pastoral office: he will share in the authority of Jesus himself. As Jesus was the Good Shepherd, so now Peter will continue the care of the sheep. The conferral of this authority upon Peter bears some resemblance to the position of Peter in the Synoptics. He is made the foundation of the Church in Matthew 16.16-19; he figures prominently in Mark and is the spokesperson for the Twelve in Mark 8. 29; in Luke Jesus tells him that he will be a fisher of men (Lk 5.10). He is mentioned first in the list of disciples and Paul tells us that the risen Lord appeared to him (1 Cor 15.5).

The editor responsible for the final chapter of John would not seek to establish the legitimacy of the ministry of Peter since this was already well-accepted in the early Church. The purpose of the inclusion of Peter in this final chapter was to give an interpretation of this existing ministry traced to Peter. The presentation of circumstances which marked the investiture of the first pastor reminds the Church for all times of the fundamental elements that must be present for the proper exercise of this ministry.

Jesus questions Peter specifically and repeats his question three times. The first condition for ministry is the love of Jesus. The triple repetition of the question may well have the triple denial of Peter in the background, but the meaning of the question and the ordering in the dialogue demands special attention. "Feed my sheep" is joined with "Do you love me?" The latter is the condition of the former.

The following dialogue discussing the Beloved Disciple further elaborates the conditions of the ministry of Peter. If Peter is willing to give his life for Jesus then he can be the shepherd of the flock. Previously in this gospel the Lord had commanded his followers to give their lives for the brethren (Jn 15.12-14) as the condition for being a disciple. Now Jesus calls upon Peter to be willing to die for him if Peter will exercise a role of leadership in the community.

The author does not invent this ministry for Peter. Jesus authenticated this office and gave the prince of the apostles a share in his own authority. The author does not engage in a polemic against Peter but rather presents an historical remembrance of the conditions upon which this ministry is based. Jesus chose Peter to share in his own task of guiding the sheep, and thus the authority of Peter is not absolute. Jesus still remains the model shepherd to whom the Father has entrusted the sheep and no one can take this away from him.

Historically we cannot verify the historicity of this event but, at least in the mind of the author, authority in the Christian community must be related to the love of Jesus even to the point of dying for Jesus and thus for the brethren. A pastoral ministry unknown in the body of the Gospel of John but evidently part of the early Church, as witnessed in the other New Testament writings, forms the heart of the Gospel of John.

THE BELOVED DISCIPLE IN JOHN 21
The Beloved Disciple also received an office in this chapter: the office of testimony. He appears with Peter, who had been given an ecclesial function, and he seems to have his own purpose in the Church. He bears testimony to Jesus

and his testimony is true (Jn 21.24). If the Beloved Disciple's testimony is authentic, he must have enjoyed a privileged position with Jesus. Both the scene at the Last Supper and at Calvary bear witness to this intimacy. The ecclesial function in this final chapter is to bear witness to the revelation of Jesus. As the intimate of the Lord his witness has value and must be considered by the community. If the Gospel of John authentically continues to preserve the heritage of the Beloved Disciple, then the Church must accept this particular testimony as part of the Jesus tradition.

PETER AND THE BELOVED DISCIPLE

Peter and the Beloved Disciple appear side by side in this final chapter, each with his own responsibility. The authority of Peter is accepted. The chapter also contains a possible reference to the death of the Beloved Disciple (Jn 21. 23). As long as the Beloved Disciple was alive the community could feel secure in its approach to Christianity. They possessed authentic Jesus traditions and lived according to the interpretation given by their founder, an intimate of the Lord. With the death of the founder the Johannine community could decide to maintain its separate existence or it could become more united to the general Christian tradition developing in the other churches. The editor of this chapter would not reject the authority of Peter, but would remind the other churches of the importance of the testimony of the beloved Disciple. The final chapter was written to emphasize the contribution of the Beloved Disciple and thus the contribution of the Johannine community to Christianity. We know that the Johannine community ceased to exist by the early second century. We also know that eventually this document was accepted by orthodox Christianity even while it was used by the heretical gnostics. Once it became part of the authentic Christian tradition, the Beloved Disciple and his community could continue their function in Christianity: they could bear witness to the Church of the approach contained in the Gospel of John. Christianity would never be a monolith as long as the Gospel of John existed and was read. Jesus gave to the Beloved Disciple the office of witness. He continues this function in the gospel that bears the name of John.

SUGGESTIONS FOR REFLECTION

1. Authority in the Church often has problems. What value does this final chapter offer in understanding the function of Church authority?

2. Is the context of pastoral authority in this chapter realistic or is it the idealization of something that could never produce the necessary control?

3. What value does the Johannine witness to faith in Jesus offer the contemporary Church? Is it really so different from the other gospels and writings of the New Testament?

4. How can the testimony of the Beloved Disciple continue in the Church? Can this aid the local Church as well as the universal Church? How can this testimony affect parochial life?

5. Why might the central authority of the Church have found difficulty in accepting the Gospel of John as authentic? Why would the gnostics have taken this gospel as their own?

6. Is there always a controversy between a more charismatic approach to Christianity and a more hierarchical and authoritarian approach? How might both approaches function to enrich the Church?

7. Do you feel comfortable with the testimony of the Beloved Disciple or not?

CHAPTER XI

THE VALUE OF THE GOSPEL OF JOHN FOR THE CONTEMPORARY CHURCH

Society often vacillates between individualism and collectivism. In most periods of history the extremes are not so evident as the pendulum continues its swing. In the recent past, however, the emphasis on individualism has waxed strong in Western countries. People live their own lives, "do their own thing" based on personal need, and often without any consideration of the needs of others. What the individual wants automatically becomes good for the community.

In religion people are also encouraged to make a personal commitment to some ideal and live accordingly. Some movements, e.g., the charismatic, encourage Christians to make a personal commitment to Jesus as a personal savior. Individuals become aware of their need to relate to Jesus on a deeply personal level and grow in the awareness of salvation as actually experienced; they are baptized in the Spirit and know that the Lord has taken a personal interest in their lives. Jesus knows each by name, calls them to himself and promises the joys that only a personal commitment can create.

Within Roman Catholicism the age of individualism has also made its mark. Church officials often seem to be defending the rights and the authority of the Church in light of the demands of individual members of the Church. Many Roman Catholics consider their consciences as the judges of morality even when their personal conclusions differ substantially from what has been the official and historical position of the Church. The individual considers his or her conscience the final decision.

The reactions of individuals, both as members of society and as members of the Church, result in no small part from an over-emphasis on the collectivity that had characterized both society and the Church for a long period. The reaction should have been expected and ultimately may contribute to a more balanced approach.

In Christianity, especially Roman Catholicism, the community was the fundamental element. Theology was developed on the concept of a common good. Directives, rules and regulations were universal in scope and application. A person could freely choose to be part of the group, but once a part, had to accept what was imposed from outside or from above. Uniformity in doctrine imposed uniformity in thought and practice. The Roman Church may never have been in theory a monolith, but in practice it surely functioned that way.

The primacy of the group over the individual produced many unfortunate results. Intellectual activity was stifled; adults were treated as children; regulations did not consider changes in society or different cultures; opportunities for enrichment were lost. When some people became aware of their personal needs, they found it impossible to remain within the Church community and left.

The Church has always suffered or gained from societal influences. If society functioned with an overdose of collectivity, the Church would feel the effects of such force in its own structure and practice. In fact, the Roman Catholic Church encouraged such attitudes and increased their strength. The structure of the Church, with its concentration of power in the hierarchy, heightened the tendency to control individuals and treat them as only parts of the whole.

The causes and sources for the current unrest that erupted at the Vatican Council may be more numerous and more intangible than historians can enumerate, but certainly part of the unrest was due to the emphasis on the collectivity, especially by the leaders of the Church and the failure on the part of the Church to deal effectively with the hopes and expectations and needs of the individual believer. For too long the person was lost in the sea of bureaucracy. Finally, people decided to make their presence and needs known.

As might be expected, all of the problems did not disappear with the advent of individualism. Perhaps we have only shifted from one set of problems to another, both of which are detrimental to the position of Christianity and its mission. The tension remains in society as well as in the Church. Should the individual be primary or not? Must the needs of the community override the needs of the person at least in some circumstances? How can the Church be true to its own structure and still allow for the needs of the individual within the Church? Is it possible for the Church to maintain a creative tension between the individual and the community, with each interacting and finding a resolution that will encourage the individual and at the same time not harm the broader needs of the Church community and structure?

The study of the Gospel of John will not solve all of the above problems facing the Church but can offer some guidance. If the gospel shows indications of a similar struggle in the early Church, and if the gospel remains for us the Word of God, then the contemporary Church may find in this document some insights into the problems and their solutions even if we have to learn to live with a perennial tension.

The gospel stresses a personal relationship to Jesus. Before all else the individual must make a faith commitment to the Lord. The study of Johannine christology shows how essential the response is, if we are to have the beginning of what we call the community of Jesus, the Church. The position of individuals in this gospel adds additional weight to the argument that the author was struggling with the need to emphasize the role and place of the individual believer for the good of the Church.

The Johannine community also wished to place the sacraments, which belong to both the group and the individual, in their proper perspective. Ritual means nothing unless it expresses the faith of committed people.

The Christian community will remain together based upon this common faith and impelled by this faith into a profound love of the brethren. The need for a love of the brethren further emphasizes that faith without the fruit of love destroys the initial faith.

In the course of history the Church as an organized community forgot or at times overlooked the need for a sure foundation in personal faith and mutual love of the brethren. The gospel calls for a return to the roots. Christianity will die if based only on organization, control and order. When the community settles for a ritual that has become formalized and fails to encourage and accept the faith commitment of its members upon which the ritual is based, then the Church teeters on the brink of destruction. When Church authority fails to consider the needs, hopes, and expectations of the individual members, then that authority is suspect. The Johannine community knew too well the pitfalls that other Christian communities experienced and tried to bear witness in its gospel to the basic elements of Christian faith.

The rights, needs, and expectations of the individual can never be overlooked by the community. Some may doubt, some lack understanding, some are impetuous and even fail in faith for a time. Jesus accepts them all and calls them to fidelity, for he is willing also to accept their failure and sins and offer forgiveness. We have examples of strong faith in this gospel: Mary and the Beloved Disciple. These are ideals, and on such ideals the Church will be secure. The community must appreciate the problems that people face without the need to render judgment and condemnation.

The Johannine community, struggling with certain aspects of the then-developing Church, did not oppose authority or an organized and hierarchical Church. Evidently some people traced their authority to Peter and to Jesus. The finai editor recognized the legitimacy of such authority but carefully reminded the Church of the context within which the authority should be exercised.

From the perspective of the twentieth century we can recognize that Christianity could have survived in an evil world only with some organization and authority. The Johannine community also recognized such a need as evidenced in the final chapter. Someone had to have authority for the community, and at times the needs of the individual must cede to the good of the whole. No single person could claim to have an absolute right *vis-à-vis* the community even though that community depended on the individuals for its existence.

The community was aware of the necessity of a communal life as evidenced in the stories about the shepherd and the flock and the vine and the branches. The command of Jesus to love the brethren also witnessed the need for a mutual relationship among the members. The tension experienced in the life style of the community as it encountered other expressions of Christianity encouraged the Johannine Church to maintain the fundamental principles upon which they had based their following of Jesus and also allowed them to admit the presence of a hierarchical and authoritarian Church. The gospel preserves the rights of the individual without denying the purpose or reality of the community. It accomplished this by stressing what is fundamental for the life of the community and placing some of the communal elements in their proper perspective.

The contemporary Church still faces similar problems that were experienced at the end of the first century. In the past, conveniently, the Church stressed the role of collectivity, but in a changed world order, it can no longer just repeat the decisions and activity of the past. Decrees, regulations, organization, and control mean nothing unless they rest upon a fundamental faith commitment to the Lord and a profound love of the brethren. This holds for all, especially for those who are leaders in the Church. The world pays attention when the Church proclaims the heart of Christianity in its structures. Whatever will build up that faith commitment and strengthen the bond of mutual love among the brethren must be the concern for the whole Church.

Some individuals in the Church may at times become so impressed by the power of faith and love that they will tend to overlook the necessity of good order and will lack the concern for the daily operation of an organization that includes 720 million people. Even so, they must be allowed their rightful place in the community so that the testimony of the Johannine community can continue to find adherents. They will stand as beacons to the Church, reminding and even chiding their brethren if necessary, to hold on to the foundations of faith and love.

For individual members of the Church the gospel offers support for a renewal in faith with the injunction that this alone is primary, but without undermining the presence and needs of the community. The individual does not hold an exclusive mandate nor may the community exercise an absolute control.

Historically we know that the enthusiasts of the Church have called this gospel their own just as the gnostics in the second century used this document as their private possession. Historically we also know that those responsible for Church order have tended to call the Gospel of Matthew, Luke/Acts and the pastoral epistles their special mandate. Any choice of one work in the New Testament as an exclusive guide invites disaster. We possess the Word of God addressed to us in the words that comprise one Bible. The Church rests upon a living of the Bible and not one book of that Bible. If the present Church turns to the witness of the Johannine community and recognizes in this writing an expression of age-old questions and some possible responses, the Church will recognize how a particular book can be of greater help at one moment in history than another.

The testimony of the Beloved Disciple and the Johannine community continues today. It will remain until the Lord returns. It was written that you may believe and may continue to believe that "Jesus is the Messiah, the Son of God, so that through this faith you may have life in his name" (Jn 20. 31).

SUGGESTIONS FOR REFLECTION

1. The conflict between individualism and the group often characterizes society as well as the Church. Does the conflict still exist in society and in the Church? Is this helpful or not?

2. If Roman Catholics make their own decisions based on conscience, how does this affect authority in the Church? Does the Gospel of John offer any guidance?

105

3. What is the value of rules and regulations in the Church? How would the Johannine community react to such control? Is there any way the Church can avoid such rules?

4. Would the Johannine community have felt at home at the Vatican Council or not? What aspects of the conciliar reform would the Johannine community have favored? What aspects would they have opposed?

5. When should the needs of the Christian community override the needs of the individual and vice versa?

6. If the early Church had such struggles, can we ever expect the struggles to end? What can be done in the meantime when we face these problems?

7. Will stressing the need of a personal relationship to the Lord assist in the problems of the contemporary Church? How might this help?

8. Will the love of the brethren radicalize the community? Is this realistic or not? How can a typical parish live such an ideal?

9. How can the concept of Church authority be altered? Or does it need to be altered? Does this gospel give any guidance for solving the problem?

SUGGESTIONS FOR FURTHER READING

Raymond E. Brown. *The Gospel According to John.* New York: Doubleday, 1966.

_____. *The Community of the Beloved Disciple.* New York: Paulist, 1979.

Robert Kysar. *John, the Maverick Gospel.* Atlanta: Knox, 1976.

_____. *The Fourth Evangelist and his Gospel.* Minneapolis: Augsburg, 1975.

Barnabas Lindars. *The Gospel of John.* Greenwood: Attic Press, 1972.

J. Louis Martyn. *The Gospel of John in Christian History.* New York: Paulist, 1979.

_____. *History and Theology in the Fourth Gospel.* Nashville: Abingdon, 1979.

Pheme Perkins. *The Gospel According to St. John.* Chicago: Franciscan Herald Press, 1978.

Stephen Smalley. *John — Evangelist and Interpreter.* Exeter: Paternoster Press, 1978.

Michael J. Taylor, ed. *A Companion to John.* New York: Alba House, 1977.